George Negus is one of Australian television's most respected journalists and popular personalities. Apart from his well-known television current affairs pedigree (*This Day Tonight*, *60 Minutes*, *Foreign Correspondent*), he has independently produced documentaries on Russia and children's rights, served on various boards and committees, including the Australian Broadcasting Tribunal's Violence Inquiry, the Federal Government's Environmental Futures Group, the Order of Australia Committee, Soccer Australia and LandCare, and made innumerable television guest appearances on everything from *The Mike Walsh Show* to *The Panel*. He is currently the host of ABC TV's popular *Australia Talks* program.

Negus is the author of *Across the Red Unknown* and *By George!*, and co-authored a bestselling children's book series, *Trev the Truck*, with his partner, Kirsty Cockburn. Cockburn, an accomplished journalist and photographer, took the cover photo and the other original photos featured in this book.

GEORGE
NEGUS

the world from
ITALY

Football, Food and Politics

HarperCollins*Publishers*

HarperCollins*Publishers*

First published in Australia in 2001
Reprinted in 2001 (five times)
This edition published in 2002
by HarperCollins*Publishers* Pty Limited
ABN 36 009 913 517
A member of the HarperCollins*Publishers* (Australia) Pty Limited Group
http://www.harpercollins.com.au

HarperCollins*Publishers*
25 Ryde Road, Pymble, Sydney NSW 2073, Australia
31 View Road, Glenfield, Auckland 10, New Zealand
77–85 Fulham Palace Road, London W6 8JB, United Kingdom
Hazelton Lanes, 55 Avenue Road, Suite 2900, Toronto, Ontario M5R 3L2
and 1995 Markham Road, Scarborough, Ontario M1B 5M8 Canada
10 East 53rd Street, New York NY 10022, USA

National Library of Australia Cataloguing-in-Publication data:

Negus, George.
    The world from Italy: football, food and politics.
    ISBN 0 7322 7457 5.
    1. Italy – Description and travel. 2. Italy – Politics and
    government. 3. Italy – Social conditions. I. Title.
914.5

Cover and internal photography by Kirsty Cockburn, except where indicated
Cover design by Luke Causby, HarperCollins Design Studio
Printed and bound in Australia by Griffin Press on 79gsm Bulky Paperback White

7 6 5 4 3 2 1   02 03 04 05

To my three darlings who were prepared to have their own lives stuffed around so that yours truly — *babbo* as he quickly became in Toscana — could fulfil his ageing adolescent dream to 'pretend he was Italian — at least for a while'. It's easy to love someone at their best; you even manage it at my worst. Wherever we are, you are my world!

Also to all of our wonderfully real, not pretend Italian friends in San Giovanni Valdarno, Strada, Firenze, Francavilla al Mare, Roma and elsewhere in *bellissima Italia*! If the post-communist world could do with a Third Way to go about things political and economic — and you only have to have half a brain to realise that it does — despite appearances to the contrary (and the *mafiosi*!), your conspicuously 'Italian way' wouldn't be the worst template!

Contents

PART ONE

ITALY OR THE BUSH?

'What do we find in Italy that can be found nowhere else? I believe it is a certain permission to be human that other countries lost long ago. Not only is Italy one of the few places left where fantasy runs unfettered — as Luigi Barzini said in *The Italians*, "even instruments of precision like speedometers and clocks are made to lie in Italy for your happiness" — it is also one of the few places that tolerates human nature with all its faults. Italy is the past, but it's also the future. It is pagan, but it is also Christian and Jewish. It is grand and tawdry, imperishable and decayed. Italy has seen marauding armies, Fascists and Communists, fashions and fripperies come and go. And it is, for all its layers of musty history, a place that embraces existence, burnishes the moment.'

Erica Jong, *My Italy*

'In Italy, you can change everything and everyone — except Italians!'

Italian journalist Indro Montanelli

The Best Question Any Journalist Can Ask — 'Why?'

Trust the Italians, in their own delightful way, to confuse the issue. Their word for 'why' is *perché*. It's one of the first words you learn as you muddle your way through the early pages of *The Complete Idiot's Guide to Teaching Yourself Italian*. They also use the same word for 'because', an instantly apparent contradiction that only the perspicacious Italians could possibly justify. But could they be onto something? The yin and yang of language perhaps? Or even the yin and yang of a lot more than just language?

This curious thought struck me back home in Australia in late 1998 when, with great monotony, friends and acquaintances were asking more or less the same quite reasonable question. *Why?* Why shoot through from the legendary Lucky Country, from God's own paradise, even for a limited period? After all, if you believe most Australians, it's the greatest bloody joint on the face of the Earth. If you have to leave at all, why Europe? And of all the places the

3

remarkable continent of Europe has to offer, why Italy, widely regarded as one of the world's more unaccomplished shambles? As a professional question-asker and political journalist, I had to admit they weren't a bad set of questions. On the other hand, the answers — most of them opening with *perché* — could leave a sufficiently large number of one-eyed Australiaphiles offended enough for them to demand my family and I hand in our cherished and heavily stamped Australian passports.

To be absolutely honest, the *combinazione* of Italian food, wine, music, art, architecture, language, people and *calcio*, football, that astonishingly ubiquitous global game at the very heart of Italian life, love, politics and culture, just might have helped decide where to base ourselves for a year to get my journalistic head into a different space.

At the risk of upsetting only about ninety per cent of the Australian population, Australia is not the greatest country on Earth. *Perché?* No country is. Claiming that your homeland is the greatest is a pretty stupid assertion to make about any place, including, if not particularly, Australia. Don't get me wrong. As a country and a place to put down roots, Australia has positive, commendable, unique, even enviable qualities almost too numerous to contemplate. But it also has plenty of ordinary, negative and occasionally objectionable ones.

Of course, you could find these same paradoxes in any of the world's myriad self-styled nations. And that includes the big ones, the small ones, the black ones, the white ones, Christian, Buddhist, Taoist, Muslim, democratic or otherwise. Basically, homo sapiens of every national persuasion are still trying, via their various idiosyncratic customs, to make sense out of the daily nonsense we laughingly call life.

Maybe that's the point. As 19-or-so-million geographically isolated Australians, we have our own ideas of how we should go about things — political, social, economic, cultural and religious. And they — the other 6.08 billion — have theirs. Like them, or significant chunks of them, we can be just as racist, sexist, naïve, ignorant, unequal, intolerant, unfair, narrow-minded and short-sighted as any other mob. Like the rest of the world, we have our own identifiable pluses and reluctantly acknowledged minuses. But for whatever set of strangely chauvinistic reasons we've always had this peculiar, almost pathological, need to keep telling ourselves and anyone else who'll listen that we are the greatest.

In the ultimate analysis, perhaps this collective Australian hang-up about how good we are in international terms comes down to the fine line between great and greatest, a line we haven't yet worked out. 'National and cultural insecurity' is a phrase that springs to mind.

Take, for instance, our distinctly Australian attitude towards politics and politicians. Wherever it may be and how well or how badly it is practised, politics is ultimately about how human beings live and how we make sense out of the nonsense I have alluded to above. But to most adult

Australians, politics is, at best, bloody boring. At worst, it's nothing more than an irritating intruder in our daily lives, something that forces us to make a detour on the way to the supermarket or the footy one Saturday every three years or so to make a mark on a ballot paper — be it formally or informally — so that we don't incur the wrath of the authorities and cop a fine.

Pollie-bashing — A National Sport!

The horrible truth is that politically Australia is probably nowhere near as sophisticated, let alone mature, as many of the less developed countries of the old 'Third World'. Admittedly, many of the grubby little dictators of the Third World do make a habit of knocking off their political opponents in awfully nasty fashion. On the other hand, we Australians are far more humane. We kill our pollies off slowly and painfully by verbally bashing them into comparative insignificance.

Our political education over the past few generations has been so inadequate that we don't actually see our elected representatives as representatives of *us*. We elect them to our three levels of government, local, State and Federal, knowing them to be ordinary, fallible, imperfect human beings. But then when we give them the dubious epithet MP, we dehumanise them. We expect them to suddenly become supermen and superwomen. Somehow we don't see bagging them as tantamount to bagging ourselves. Ipso facto, if democracy — that word we all bandy about with reckless abandon — means anything at all, that's what it must mean. We are them; they are us. We elect them; they represent us. Collectively, they are no better or worse than the rest of us. But depending on our self-interest levels, we want them to be both: better than us when we need them and worse than us for the rest of the time.

We're shocked that the calibre and standing of our MPs is so low while at the same time we never seem to tire of writing them off as either crooks or morons. More often, we treat them like scum and vermin and then expect them to thank us for electing them and rush off to simultaneously do both our individual bidding and the proverbial Right Thing by the nation. We carry on about how in the long run 'they're all the bloody same' or 'they're as bad as each other'. 'No matter who you vote for a blasted politician always wins' is the too-smart-by-half Australian lament. Then we grumble that there's no real choice between the values and ideologies of the major parties.

Ultimately this amounts to a fairly ordinary excuse for a massive political cop-out. What better way to not want to or not be able to make up our minds about what we think is important, let alone what set of social and economic values the country should be run on, than to claim that we have no real ideological choice? We *do* have a choice. We just don't want to make it. Maybe we should save ourselves the trouble of voting and just toss a coin every three years or so to see which side gets to form government. It makes as much sense as voting one way or the other without quite knowing why!

As a defrocked, sunstruck, sub-tropical Queenslander, I grew up being told by my elders not to talk about sex, religion and politics. They 'make bad friends', everyone from granny to the local footy coach told us ad nauseam. What they never got around to explaining was what *did* make good friends. At the age of about eighteen, I discovered that sex, religion and politics were about the only things worth arguing about and I haven't stopped arguing about them since.

So what does this harangue in defence of politics and politicians got to do with my going off to Europe for what I've been calling a working sabbatical, a burst of personal battery recharging? For a long time I'd wondered what it would be like to live and work for a while in a social environment in which politics and politicians were not so much taken seriously as enjoyed. Somehow or other, the Europeans, especially the Italians, appear to have managed this.

Like Australians, Italians get stuck into their pollies. But out of all their regular and eloquent gum-bumping over terrific *caffè*, or an *aperitivo* or glass of *vino locale* in their favourite bar on the piazza, they have gained a political maturity. It might encompass the mad Left to the mad Right and every possible permutation and combination in between, but it's a noticeable maturity nevertheless. For most of us, dealing with politics and politicians is the ultimate love-hate relationship. Italians certainly love to hate their pollies, but they also hate to love them. We in Australia just can't stand a bar of them either way.

So why are Italians different? This book you've embarked upon is an attempt to supply at least an inkling of an answer. One early observation is that it's possible Italians don't expect too much of their pollies because they don't expect too much of themselves. Could that well be a quaintly perverted working definition of democracy itself? Don't be shocked when politicians get it wrong; be pleasantly surprised when they don't!

Italy — A Contentious Alliance of Opposites

In one of Florence's more irresistible English-language bookshops, I picked up an anthology entitled, a little too cutely for mine, *Italy in Mind*. It's a collection of works from just about anyone 'literary' — from Byron and Elizabeth Barrett Browning, through D. H. Lawrence and Herman Melville to Susan Sontag and Gore Vidal — on their respective and profoundly different love affairs with Italy. In her introduction, editor Alice Leccese Powers makes a number of interesting and colourful observations. This one caught my fancy: 'Italy is a contentious alliance of opposites — the North and the South, the Mediterranean and the Alps, the ancient and the modern, the Christian and the pagan. It encompasses crowded Neapolitan cafés and solitary Tuscan trattorias, the haunting stillness of Venetian passageways and the cacophony of Roman roundabouts; the high fashion of Milanese couture and the ubiquitous black dresses of Sicilian widows. Incongruity does not confound Italians. They thrive on chaos.' Powers seemed to be confirming my long-held views on the matter: that Italy is a land of paradox and not-so-self-evident truths.

But like so many other contemporary writers and commentators who have observed Italy in the latter half of the twentieth century and the beginning of the twenty-first, Powers left out one glaring example of what she described as 'a contentious alliance of opposites'. Consciously or otherwise, she ignored possibly Italy's most contentious alliance of opposites, the Left and the Right! What is it about politics that scares the shit out of so many writers? For me, I'm afraid I can't live, work and write in that sort of self-imposed explanation vacuum. After twenty-five years of globe-trotting and people-watching, I have come to the conclusion that this aversion makes for a very 'unhuman' view of the world, short on values and short on understanding. As a small-p political animal, I've always wanted to see the Left and Right, the ideological yin and yang, operating somewhere on a regular, natural daily basis.

It's not all that surprising that it took an Italian, Dr Roberto Nobbio, to put together a work simply called *Left and Right*. Nobbio, the supreme Italian realist-cum-idealist, goes on to debunk the 'end of history' view of the past decade or so. He argues instead that the fundamental distinction between the Left and Right, which has shaped our world since the French Revolution, is just as relevant today as it ever was. For what it's worth, I couldn't agree more. This observer would argue that just because so many of us would like to believe or have convinced ourselves that the causes of a Left-Right view of society, people and nations no longer exist, this doesn't necessarily mean they don't.

Just a Job of Journalism!

If this all sounds like an author's disclaimer, that's because it is! This is not an autobiography. Nor is it treatise. It's not really a travel book and it's definitely not one of those cloying things that every bugger who reckons he or she can string a few words together feels obliged to write about their personal experience of Italy. Nor, indeed, is it just about Italy. It is more about long-held musings and opinions sparked anew by being in a place like Italy for a period of time, being surrounded by Italians, responding to their attitudes, vulgarising their language, reading about them, socialising with them, eating and cooking their food, enjoying their football, appreciating their culture and being stirred by their slightly mad politics. Most are reactions to international, even universal issues that go way beyond Italy's magnificent geography and its multifarious society.

Tim Parks, an Englishman who for years has been well and truly ensconced in Italy with his Italian family, is one of those brave enough, or maybe silly enough, to write not one, but two non-fiction books about his Italian experiences. One is based on dealing with his neighbours in Verona and the other on his kids' schooling there. 'I swore I would never write about the place,' he wrote in *An Italian Education*, his second book. It's not coincidental that despite his reservations about writing his Italian books, both of Parks' failed attempts at non-book-writing have been bestsellers.

Parks says he has always been suspicious of travel writing, of what he dubs 'attempts to establish that elusive element which might or might not be national character, to say in sweeping and general terms, this place is like this, that place is like that'. Having read most of these Italian-inspired books either for the hell of it or as quasi-research for our family jaunt, I can only say I feel the same way. But that will not prevent the occasional sweeping statement or generalisation from finding its way into this book, hopefully not about 'elusive elements' in Italy's national character, but rather less romantic, more obvious socio-political matters, the simple yet profound things that glue Italy and Italians together, things that the rest of us might learn from.

Somehow, 'Italianness' encourages one to ponder humanness. Perhaps it's because Italians have different priorities. Perhaps their priorities, preferences and predilections are just more fundamental and obvious. Perhaps they are basically happy with what they've concluded is important — the essentials like football, food and politics — and that 'all the rest is mere detail', as a T-shirt in the famous daily market in Florence proudly declared. Or perhaps it's because Italians are so unapologetically *human* that they blatantly relish going to the football, eating food and shouting at each other about politics.

The World from Italy: Football, Food and Politics is, to some degree, an elucidation of the new evolving international ideology of the 'Third Way', being seen by many as a fresh political route the world might consider as we charge from the mildly to the wildly confused, out of the 'communism versus capitalism' contest of the twentieth century into the karmic unknown of the twenty-first.

The Third Way rejects the traditional nexus of the Left and the Right and encourages greater scepticism of — as distinct from outright opposition to — the apparently unassailable forces of globalisation and the overhyped IT revolution. Call me a heretic or just a professional observer who sees these 'neo-religions' as ultimately important yet inadequately tested tools rather than solutions, but haven't we always been warned that fanaticism in whatever narrow-minded form, whenever and from wherever it comes, is to be avoided? Surely this same age-old rule of thumb applies to the gulf between the global e-economy and real human needs and aspirations.

It's probably worth pointing out that after decades of coming to grips with the 'tic' in politics, I feel no particular need to spell out the details of this elusive Third Way. If there is a motivation, it is merely to acknowledge the screaming necessity for one. The obvious shortcomings of the existing two ways that have dominated both our pondering and practice of politics for the past three-quarters of a century are reason enough.

Right now, wherever you are — Australia, Italy, wherever — it's difficult if not impossible to fathom who's worse off: the post-communist strugglers failing to cope with the ruthlessness of the global economy or the stragglers of the New World Order falling by the wayside in their desperate scramble to stay on or even get on the 'information superhighway', a journey where the bottom line and the bottom of the barrel look frighteningly similar.

Of All People, How Could the Italians Have the Answers?

After an unbroken year living with them at close quarters, the Italians' seductive socio-economic alloy of football, food and politics began to suggest that for forty years or more, at least since the end of the Second World War, they'd been pursuing their own 'Third Way'. It might have been recently talked up by the likes of Tony Blair, Bill Clinton and Gerhard Schroeder, but the facts are that it may not be a new political idea at all. It could well be an old Italian one.

How can you not take notice of a nation led until very recently by ideological Walter Mitty, the former Communist, now reconstituted and thoroughly civilised 'Third Way' advocate, Massimo D'Alema? D'Alema, gone but not forgotten like all Italian leaders, after spending a day sailing on his favourite Gulf of Taranto and an evening watching Lecce, the local football team he supports, make its debut in Serie A, the national football league, had this to say: 'Those who say that they work all the time are show-offs. Vacations are a sign of a civilised society.'

Italians appear to agree in spades with their former prime minister. For the month of August, pretty much the entire country comes to a slumberous halt but still it manages to keep its place among the world's top five or six economic powers. In contrast, Americans are scared shitless to take off even two weeks a year. Americans also go to psychiatrists more often than Italians go to football matches, which is not easy to do! There's got to be a lesson in there somewhere.

Traveller's Magnet and Political Paradox

Italy has long been a magnet for travellers, tourists and all sorts of visitors with various motivations. Former *New York Times* bureau chief in Rome and now Italian resident Paul Hofmann listed Italy's foreign gatecrashers as follows: 'First came barbarian invaders who craved the lush South and its riches. They were followed by Saracen plunderers; northern pilgrims to the tombs of the Apostles in Rome; sages like Montaigne who toured the peninsula's spas and, "only to distract myself", made a point of looking at the courtesans in Venice, Florence and Rome; English lords on their grand tour; Goethe, Stendahl, Byron, Ruskin and Henry James; an endless line of artists from Dürer to Henry Moore; honeymooners from all over Europe and the Americas; and today's package tours from the US and Japan.'

Hofmann left out a few categories, including Australian foreign correspondents who have for years considered that Italy — whether or not it really is the disorganised shambles its many detractors paint it to be and despite what Hofmann called its 'conflicting impressions' — has something to teach the rest of us, provided we can sublimate our instinctive chauvinism long enough to take notice. Possibly it's their indefatigable gift for 'snapping back after catastrophe and for making do with whatever is at hand', as Hofmann put it.

Whatever it is, invasion, war, internal turmoil, flood, famine, earthquake, quite possibly pestilence, the Medicis, Marx, Mussolini, the Mafia, the Roman Catholic church, world records for strikes, disruption of business and industrial conflict, a paralysing bureaucracy, more revolving-door governments in the last half century than the rest of us have had decent holidays, kidnapping as an entrepreneurial activity, homicidal terrorism from both left- and right-wing extremists, and even losing football's coveted World Cup by one measly penalty kick have failed to intimidate the Italians. Any one of these calamities, let alone the historical accumulation of them, would bring most nations to their proverbial knees. Italy, on the other hand, has prospered, almost in spite of them.

It's just possible, of course, that the subtitle of this book says it all. The football is on like clockwork every weekend, the food is invariably *al dente*, and the politics, whatever else it is, is always unpredictable and never boring. Between them, these three national personality traits — stimulants to some, drugs to others — provide for heady conversation over the morning *caffè*. All the rest is mere detail!

PART TWO

FOOTBALL IS LIFE!

'For millions of Italians, Sundays are less sacred for mass in the morning than for football in the afternoon!'

Berlitz

The Buddhist and the Baron

Milan-based Silvio Berlusconi is widely known to Italians and non-Italians alike as a megalomaniacal media tycoon, a distastefully wealthy property developer, a supermarket chain-owner and an allegedly corrupt right-wing Italian politician. For a heady interval back in the mid 1990s, he was also the elected Italian Prime Minister. Today, he is in political relapse as Italy's tacit Opposition Leader, though he is widely tipped to win Italy's general elections in April 2001.

Roberto Baggio, meanwhile, is widely known as an uncommonly eccentric, pony-tailed, mountain-trekking Buddhist, a media-made sex symbol and a highly marketable Italian soccer star. He's a household name with football fans around the world. Recently, their disparate lives have been inextricably linked. So what, you might ask, could an ambitious magnate like Berlusconi and Baggio, a near-legendary *calciatore*, possibly have in common? The answer is both peculiar and typically Italian.

In the crucial penalty shootout to decide the final of the 1994 World Cup, the world's most prestigious and widely watched sporting event, Baggio, at the time striker with the Italian national team, the *Azzurri*, smashed his match-deciding shot over the Brazilian goalkeeper's head and, to his, his Italian teammates and Italians the world over's unutterable dismay, well over the crossbar. Italy lost the World Cup.

Overnight the 'saviour', 'magician' and 'little Buddha' of Italian football went from football god to 'a wet lame rabbit', 'a sour disappointment' and 'a national failure'. In short, he copped the full rooster-to-feather-duster treatment from his formerly adoring fans. Meanwhile, Berlusconi, who, aided and abetted by his immense wealth and his commercial media outlets, had chosen to use football to enhance his popularity throughout the country and thereby shore up his political fortunes, lost a well-planned opportunity to burgle the country's prime ministership.

When the BBC's Rome correspondent, Matt Frei, wrote about this moment in *Italy: The Unfinished Revolution*, he confirmed the notion that Italians are 'ruthless with losers, especially in politics and soccer'. Indeed, as Frei and others, including myself, are convinced, if Baggio had scored instead of blasting his right-foot drive over the bar, Italian political developments in the 1990s 'would have been radically different'.

How and why? Isn't it just a bit over the top to seriously suggest that a nation's government — indeed, a country's entire political future — could be so drastically affected by a missed goal in a football match? In the case of Italy, this is not really as remarkable as it might sound.

The highly unconventional vehicle that drove Berlusconi to power was Forza Italia, a carefully manufactured vote-winning machine more like a nationwide social club than a political party. Clearly anti-communist and anti-Left generally, it had neither a real ideology nor a social base. As many saw it — and they were not wrong — Forza Italia was merely a means for the commercially avaricious Berlusconi to cynically and quite unashamedly protect and promote his massive business interests. Forza Italia was not so much pro-business; it was pro-Berlusconi business. At a point in his rise to the top, Berlusconi realised it was ultimately easier, though not necessarily cheaper, to become a politician himself, even Prime Minister, than to have to lobby, cajole, threaten and influence politicians or, as was often the case in Italy's postwar Mafia-dominated political climate, even bribe them.

In its first few months of existence, Forza Italia went literally from being a non-entity in Italian politics to the country's most popular party. To get there, Berlusconi blatantly exploited Italy's 'language of football for political ends', as Frei put it. Not such a crazy idea. Indeed, in a country like Italy, it was an idea that had been waiting to happen. Italians are or have been over many decades emotionally fervent about both their soccer and their politics. They love one and love to hate the other. It is amazing that no one before the connivingly determined Berlusconi and his horde of marketing professionals had worked out a way to unite the two great Italian passions.

Not at all coincidentally, the Forza Italia social clubs that mushroomed all over Italy — 7000 of them with over 1 million paying members — were modelled on the fan clubs of the famous red-and-black-striped AC Milan, which just happened to be owned, you guessed it, by Sr. Berlusconi, the team's richest *tifoso*, fan. For 300 000 lire (around US$230), paid-up Forza Italia members got posters, rattles, ties, flags, pens — the same sort of paraphernalia footy fans around the world get when they sign up as a member of a club.

But Forza Italia members also received Berlusconi's political manifesto, inasmuch as its frighteningly simplistic right-wing ideology could be deemed a manifesto. Very basically, he was advocating what some commentators at the time labelled 'Mediterranean Thatcherism': lower taxation, the minimisation of Italy's infamous bureaucracy, practically no government interference in anything, the free-est of free markets, and that old chestnut of the Right anywhere, law and order. This last plank in the Forza Italia platform was a surefire winner in a country like Italy, for decades under the criminal yoke of the Mafia and organised crime.

The Ultimate Unholy Trinity — Business, Soccer and Politics

Through Forza Italia, business, politics and soccer in Italy had been converted into a new holy trinity with Berlusconi as 'Il Papa', AC Milan as his personally ordained church, and the country's millions of fanatical football supporters as its congregation. Enough of them signed up and enough prayers must have gone out to Mammon to lift him not to Heaven and the right hand of God, but at least immediately in front of the Speaker of the Italian Parliament as Prime Minister.

He was welcomed by many, including some who did not share his brand of pseudo-politics, as the first Italian leader in years to have little in common with either the habitually elected Christian Democrats or the motley crew of Socialists and Communists who, over a period of forty years, had opposed and occasionally defeated them.

Berlusconi made his much fanfared, self-funded entry into Italian politics with enormous help from the hugely convenient free-to-air mediums of his own three national TV channels. Matt Frei recalled that the media baron did not announce that he was entering the country's political arena. Significantly, he said he was 'taking the field' (*scendo in campo*).

Warming to his football theme, Berlusconi described Forza Italia's candidates in the election as the *Azzurri* or

'Blues', the moniker traditionally given to the country's beloved national eleven. When Berlusconi eventually made it into government, as Prime Minister, he referred to his Cabinet as *la squadra*, the team.

But Berlusconi's most unsubtle exploitation of the soccer metaphor was the name he gave to his so-called party, Forza Italia. The actual meaning is a bit imprecise, but 'Come on, Italy!' or 'Go for it, Italy!' are close enough. Every weekend, 'Forza!' is the rallying cry fans boom out almost orchestrally from the terraces of Italy's stadiums as they urge on their favourite team. For AC Milan it's 'Forza Milan!' For the national squad it is — with or without Berlusconi's influence and TV stations — 'Forza Italia!' For me and my family, de facto Tuscans and Fiorentina fans for fifteen months, it was 'Forza Viola!' Wrote Frei: 'Berlusconi had made a simple calculation. The Italians, he told himself, eat my food, they watch my television channels with their low-fibre diet of game shows, B-movies and very soft porn. Tens of thousands of them live in houses and flats that I have built, they go on holidays to the seaside resorts I have constructed, they love my football team, surely they will also worship me if I go into politics.'

He was right. In May 1994, Silvio Berlusconi became Prime Minister of Italy, despite having had no direct political experience during his extensive business life. He rode the Forza Italia wave to power. As his AC Milan club was winning Serie A matches, his political team kicked enough goals to win sufficient votes for him to get the job he wanted but didn't need.

With the Italian 1994 World Cup squad littered with AC Milan players, the Berlusconi plan was for Italy to win and for him to take over Italy. It damned near came off. As Frei recalled: 'For two weeks in the summer of 1994, as the whole country was gripped by World Cup fever, one couldn't be sure whether Italians shouting "Forza Italia!" were egging on the national team or the Prime Minister's ruling party. This was precisely the intention . . .'

But not even Berlusconi could have bargained on Roby Baggio missing that fateful penalty. 'A collective groan of despair echoed throughout the country,' wrote Frei. 'World Cup-weary Italians who had hoped to celebrate all night, lurched home, their heads bowed, their flags rolled up, their rattles silent.' Significantly, the seemingly all-conquering Forza Italia battle cry 'had begun to sound hollow in soccer and, as it turned out, in politics'.

After the World Cup disaster, the steam definitely began to run out of the Forza Italia juggernaut. But seven years later in 2001, Berlusconi still has his untold millions, still owns his league-winning AC Milan, and still retains his seat in Parliament. His newly cobbled centre-right 'Polo' group has clawed its way back in regional elections, and the prime ministership is in his sights. In September 2000, Italian Prime Minister Giuliano Amato announced that he would accede control of his centre-left government to Francesco

Rutelli, the richly charismatic mayor of Rome, in a bid to defeat the resurgent Berlusconi in the 2001 general elections. Berlusconi has produced a 25-point manifesto, which includes a proposal for coastguards to shoot at boats smuggling illegal immigrants, and has forged alliances with the neo-fascist National Alliance and the pro-secessionist Northern League. He has also successfully shrugged off most of the corruption allegations that have been made against him in the past few years.

Roby Baggio? He's still around, just as interesting as an individual and as a player, though he is no longer with Berlusconi's mighty AC Milan. For a while he languished on the bench for Inter Milan, AC Milan's crosstown rivals, watching the likes of Brazil's Ronaldo and Christian Vieri net the goals he used to put away. When he complained about not being picked, he was told by club officials to 'like it or lump it'; in other words, to maybe start looking for another club. Which he did — in September 2000 he transferred to newly promoted Serie A club Brescia in order to 'prove myself to [Italian national coach Giovanni] Trapattoni' — but only after resurrecting his career in spectacular fashion at Inter.

In 1999, in three crucial performances in the space of one week, Baggio respectively scored the match-winner against Verona; got the equaliser in the derby against AC Milan, the draw taking Inter through to the semi-finals of the Italian Cup; and against Roma the following weekend, set up the team's first goal, scored by Vieri, and then scored what one observer described as a 'magical' second goal. After the national slagging he got after missing that vital penalty at USA '94, Baggio — with 158 goals, the highest goalscorer still playing Serie A in Italy — received a thunderous standing ovation from Inter's 60 000 fickle fans. It was the stuff of sporting dreams.

The 'yin and yang' of football, perhaps?

Sport and Politics — A Distinctly Italian Concoction

There are probably only a handful of other examples in recent world history in which sport and politics have become so utterly intertwined like they were in the Baggio-Berlusconi 'one-two'. Of course, there were the protests against apartheid in South Africa back in the 1970s, when international sanctions against that country's white minority government included a ban on the famous Springboks, then a 'whites only' rugby union side. Then there was the refusal of some countries to compete in the 1980 Moscow Olympics in protest against the Soviet invasion of Afghanistan. And, of course, you could toss in the murderous bomb attack on Israeli athletes by Palestinian Al Fatah extremists during the 1972 Munich Olympics.

In Italy, however, the quarrel is not so much how to keep sport out of politics. Rather, the Italians contend that it is inevitable that sport and politics will occasionally collide in the day-to-day affairs of a country that feels so passionately about both. One San Giovannese friend — a food and wine-lover, political activist and football fan, the consummate Italian — put it in his own inimitable way. 'After all,' he told me over a pizza and a glass or two of *vino di casa*, 'all Italians vote and they all watch football. We support our preferred political party and our team. We have politicians we like and politicians we don't like. It's the same with footballers. In many ways, for Italians — whether they support Berlusconi and the Right or Massimo D'Alema and the Left, whether they shout for Fiorentina or AC Milan — it is impossible to divide the two.'

Canals, *Calcio* and Carnevale

Travelling by ferry is hardly a normal way to get to a football match or, indeed, any sporting event. Except, that is, if the journey is across Italy's Bay of Venice. For the devoted fans of AC Venezia, when their beloved Serie A *squadra* is playing at home at the Stadio di Penzo, the twenty-minute *vaporetto* (ferry) journey from historic Piazza San Marco to San Elena is standard procedure.

You'd have to say though, that even to *calcio*-mad Italians, football is not exactly a predictable event on the Venetian calendar, particularly in February during winter crush of the canal city's famous Carnevale.

With or without the Italian preoccupation with *calcio*, over a packed week-and-a-half, probably 500,000 people cross the four-kilometre causeway from horribly industrial Mestre to Venice, many of them already decked out in flamboyant medieval garb.

As the ‌‌‌‌‌‌‌‌‌‌‌‌‌‌‌‌ quite unabashed days of nihilistic 'festivity and transgression'. This makes more sense when you realise that it takes place immediately before Lent, when all things carnal and carnivorous are supposed to come to a screaming halt in 'good' Catholic countries like Italy. It dates back to the eleventh century when, of course, the power and influence of Venice as a great maritime city-state was undisputed. But twenty years ago, festivity replaced 'fastivity' and the annual Carnevale was literally recreated by the ever-inventive Venetians, most inventive, of course, when it comes to survival techniques for their drowning museum-cum-home.

No one's counting, but just about everyone knows that Venice's 117 tiny islands, 150 or so canals and staggering 400-odd bridges are under constant and unremitting threat. In actual fact, it's probably one of those rare occasions in which counting is, indeed, justified. Someone once wisecracked that mouth-to-mouth resuscitation, Venetian-style, amounts to the precarious city staying alive, physically and financially, against incredible natural and human odds — a clever way of stating the case for unavoidable commercialism. Over the years various manufactured attractions, real art and genuine history have kept the city alive and prosperous. But the real test is whether or not architectural thinking, specialist engineering ingenuity and sheer political will combine to save Venice from a grisly aquatic demise.

Whether as a traveller or a tourist — and they are definitely very different animals — it's on about the third or fourth trip that you eventually realise Venice, 'La Serenissima', a city with genuine serenity, wouldn't exist if you and your fellow credit card-wielders were not there. As Mary McCarthy, whose *Venice Observed* is regarded as something of a contemporary classic, said, there's 'no use in pretending that the tourist Venice is not the real Venice'. But as one of that handful of special places in the world for which the tag 'unique' is not an exaggerated adornment but thoroughly appropriate, that's easy to live with.

But back to that jam-packed *vaporetto*. On the proverbial Venetian morning after the Saturday night before, and with small-c Catholic carnevale confessions out of the way for those distracted enough to aspire to eternal life, thousands of conscious transgressors, mainly blokes in what is still largely an unliberated Italy, turned to that other undying Italian passion-cum-art form, *calcio*.

Out came the Sunday best for the annual clash on the lagoon between the home side Venezia and their age-old rivals from the capital, AS Roma. Speaking as an observer only of things sartorial, Italian football followers have got to be the best-dressed sports fans in the world. That chic haberdasher's term 'smart casual', somewhere between a sports jacket and whatever, was invented for them — if not by them. Not just the more expensively ticketed stands, but also the open, windy terraces at Stadio Pierluigi Penzo were tier-to-tier suede, leather, Armani, Versace and Missoni. Jeans, cords, waisted jackets or sweaters, all the boys were on the to-be-seen-in, not the just-to-be-worn bandwagon. They even scrubbed up nicely in trackies; the upmarket Sergio Tacchini variety, it has to be said. As for the footwear of the Italian fans, they wear the sort of stuff we might pull on for a night out at a fancy restaurant.

Later we were to discover, to the horror and shame of our modest traveller's wardrobe, that it wasn't just to Serie A matches that the good gear came out. Even at our thirteen-year-old son's *partita di calcio* in our totally non-touristy 'hometown' of San Giovanni Valdarno, we were well down the fashion pecking order. But our fellow spectators seemed to understand. After all, we weren't Italian — just pretending for a while!

But in Venice that day, we couldn't have been anywhere but Italy. Where else would two football teams leave the players' race and take the field to the rousing operatic strains of Verdi? What's more, the Roma and Venezia 'boys' behind the goals at both ends of the pitch knew all the words and sang along — in tune as much as I could tell! After all, Italian football is pure theatre. The night before, the wildly thronging Piazza San Marco had produced impromptu Carnevale street theatre. On this day, Stadio Pierluigi Penzo orchestrated its own kind of carnival — the flares, the flags, the chorus, the eurhythmy of the chanting and clapping of *calcio*.

So What's Behind the Mask?

In the eighteenth century, Venice was regularly invaded by self-styled gentlemen and ladies from all over Europe, hellbent on enjoying themselves in most ungentlemanly and unladylike fashion. As they cavorted along its *calli*, *piazze*, casinos, theatres and bedrooms, their modesty, reputation and morality was protected and/or elaborately disguised in traditional top-to-toe garb. And so it is today, as far as I could make out, possibly with a little less public cavorting.

Nevertheless, Jan Morris, in *The World of Venice*, was utterly convinced that 'there is sex and susceptibility in the very air of the place as any ravished alien will attest'. Never having been a ravished alien in Venice, I'm nonetheless certainly susceptible enough to acknowledge that the showy salaciousness of Venice at Carnevale could raise erotic hopes, if not serious possibilities. Maybe there's a fine line between the sought-after courtesans of Venice's colourful Renaissance past and the callgirls and escort services of today. Reading Morris, I was interested to discover that in other times the Church had 'an easygoing attitude towards the libertines' of Venice.

Morris also revealed, to my non-Catholic mortification, that in the chapel of San Clemente in the marvellous basilica of San Marco, scandalous things had transpired between gay young nuns and their visitors. Having recovered from the shock of discovering that gay young nuns were not merely the stuff of porn rag fantasies, it was time to get back to the look-only loose living of Carnevale.

As time passed, we're told, so too did Renaissance-like tolerance towards Feb-*festa* sex and once-a-year promiscuity. 'Aristocratic privilege lost ground to subversive notions of hygiene and democracy', is *Desiring Italy* author Susan Cahill's sweep of Venetian history. If the famously lascivious Lord Byron were to show up at today's Carnevale, Cahill says he would 'find the new women sketched by Jan Morris disappointing, if not infuriating'.

Nevertheless, over the last century or so, undaunted by time or fad and aided and abetted by the city's noted maskmakers, the mystery of the mask, from the elegantly alluring to the outrageous bird-like proboscis, has become the Carnevale's beguiling symbol of liberation. For ten days leading up to Ash Wednesday, *maschere e mascherieri* — masks and maskmakers — are everywhere in the city of canals. It's impossible to take a *macchiato*, sip a *vino rosso*, tuck into a *fegato di Venezia* or cross the Rialto Bridge without literally bumping into masked revellers. Faceless, they parade their anonymity, posing, primping, showing off. The odd ones out in Venice in early February are definitely the unmasked.

The famous annual *festa* is not, of course, restricted to Venice. Most of Italy has its local adaptation. Italian journalist Stefano Salimbeni put it in perspective when he said that it's all 'part of the temporary madness across the nation that characterises Carnevale'.

'From tomorrow until next Tuesday,' Salimbeni wrote, 'Italy will celebrate what is probably the oldest festivity it observes. Virtually every community in the country will host its own version of this whirlwind of costumes and practical jokes, parades, dances, music, street performances, food — especially the fried and sugary kinds — and the inevitable flood of wine.'

Carnevale, they say, is about the 'victory of the light of spring over the darkness of winter'. Without putting too fine a point on it, it's yet another of those usually unsuccessful attempts to tame the eternal struggle between good and evil — whatever they are. It's this unbridled yet peaceful gaiety that's the real origin of Carnevale, the resurrection of old pagan winter rites 'when disguises and laughter were used to chase away evil spirits', as Salimbeni puts it. The ancient Romans called it Saturnalia. The modern Romans have their contemporary version.

In this national long weekend of partying, Venice, however, remains Italy's carnival showcase. From the classy to the over-the-top, it has become an institution and in the rare quieter *calli* near Piazza San Margherita, Campo San Polo and even Accademia, a haunt for the pretentiously unpretentious.

Meanwhile, back on the lagoon, with mastheads bobbing above the low eastern terrace and a church spire towering behind reminding us all, if we had any doubts, that this was a truly bizarre venue for a football match, the Venetians were doing better at the Stadio di Penzo than the Christians used to do against the lions at the Colosseum. The result — Venezia 3 Roma 1 — was a serious turn-up. The masked Carnevale revellers were not the only ones disguising their real feelings that festival weekend. Loyal Venetian *amatori del calcio*, football lovers, were also hiding something beneath their smart but less flamboyant wardrobe, not the indiscretions of the previous night, but more than a little surprise and pent-up delight that their local underdogs had taken out the powerful Romans.

Where 'incomparable Venice' is concerned — as Sophia Loren, another incomparable Italian monument once drooled — with all the silky praise comes damnation. Forget all those self-evident truths about the state of the canals, including, if not especially, the great Grande itself. The whole place cops it!

What is it, I've found myself asking over decades of travel from the most glorious to the most appalling destinations, that encourages commentators to denounce places and situations that are fundamentally extraordinary? Maybe it has something to do with some primeval need to be part of the pack, but, at the same time, keeping a safe distance from it.

By any measure, Venice is a mindblowing place. Indeed, as cities go, it's not just a city. It's *Venice*, a marvellously messy labyrinth of *canali*, *ponti* and *palazzi* — canals, bridges and palaces — literally propped up on pylons of sticks. It hangs there in such adroit fashion that somehow, despite centuries of tides, floods and a constant human deluge, it's still there for anyone with an airfare, bus or train ticket to enjoy. It defies gravity, commonsense and reason. It's part of a past that refuses to be swallowed up by the future except on its own idiosyncratic terms. And even though its very existence depends on defying the ravages of time and deterioration, it stays afloat regardless of a multitude of reasons why it shouldn't.

Exceptional or otherwise, like that other extraplanetary metropolis, New York, you have to *go* with Venice. You have to become a temporary Venetian, as you must become a temporary New Yorker, otherwise it will depress and frustrate you. No choice. Venice makes the rules, you follow them. And who could possibly object to being led by Venice? Geographically, physically, topographically, let alone notionally, it is not of this world.

A Place Where Anyone Can Walk on Water

If you believe Susan Cahill, people actually try to lose themselves in Venice's watery confusion. 'There's a desire to get lost,' she says. 'The pleasure of the place is the maze itself, not be to figured out!' Not everyone who's completely lost their way in Venice would be all that convinced about the maze being entirely pleasurable, but if you've been even half-lost in Venice, you know only too well what Cahill's getting at — fun and frustration complementing each other in just about equal measure.

One night, late, I walked — ran — back to a quaint trattoria in the slightly less-touristy San Polo neighbourhood where my family and I had eaten and where I had carelessly left a small backpack of traveller's valuables. On my rapid, nervous foot slog back to our out-of-the-way eatery, I could have been anywhere. Venice had vanished. The reality of my potential loss had replaced the surreality of where I was. To my relief, the backpack was there, safe behind the cash register where the friendly waiter had put it to await my return. I got the distinct impression from his polite, somewhat patronising manner that maybe we weren't the first absentminded fly-by-nighters he'd come across.

The walk back through the Campo di Santa Margherita and the Accademia district to our *pensione* near San Marco was altogether different. This time, at ease and taking my time, I actually noticed nocturnal Venice — the half-light, half-dark, the human and still-life shadows, the shapes, the buildings, the pavements, the bridges, the lampposts, the water in the canals, its non-pristine condition an irrelevance at that near-bewitching hour. Now that my own heart had ceased to beat like a snare drum, I heard Venice — the footsteps other than my own, a far-off jazz band, Vivaldi coming from somewhere, pop schmaltz from a back-canal teen haunt and, of course, the bells. And every few metres, people — couples, small groups, all laughing, mostly masked, needless to say — broke the quietude more loudly than either my hurried footsteps or the music.

Christ may or may not have walked on water, but in Venice, even mere mortals get carried around by its omnipresence. That night on the other side of the Grand Canal, it would have been a crime to walk quickly, to not see and hear. In the same way, it would be a crime if La Serenissima sank and drowned — as many still fear it will — before other dreamers can enjoy the same walk and hear the same sounds. Jan Morris' explanation of Venice euphoria is to suggest that it is 'less a city and more an experience'. The less romantic, more sceptical line is that it would, indeed, be a sin not to protect and preserve this place, not for artistic or cultural reasons, not even for architectural ones, but simply because Venice is *there*.

Some fifteen years ago I put together a report for Australian television on what might be done to hold back the tidal and rain waters in the Bay of Venice and stop the city of canals from literally drowning. At the time, an international marine engineering competition had been launched to find a way around the problem.

The leading contender had a bold idea based on raising gigantic inflatable barricades to control the increased flows that periodically threaten the Piazza San Marco, the Bridge of Sighs — indeed, the entire magnificence that is Venezia. Today that project — or one very much along the same lines and principles — is still on the city's political agenda. They've given it a thoroughly appropriate Biblical name. It's been dubbed 'Moses', after the Old Testament prophet who, of course, held back the waters of the Red Sea. Ostensibly a collection of huge portable dykes, the 'Moses' project, if it ever goes ahead, is estimated to cost 5 trillion lire, but it has stalled. No Venetian politician has been prepared to bite the politico-economic bullet needed to get it off the drawing board and down onto the sandy bottom of the notoriously fickle Bay of Venice.

Early in 2000, the centre-left Mayor of Venice, philosophy professor and 'most fascinating man in Italy' (according to a women's magazine poll) Massimo Cacciari, resigned, apparently in a fit of pique. He spat the mayoral dummy during yet another heated council debate over the project. 'Water Politics Intensify As Venice Mayor Resigns' was the headline in the *Italy Daily*. It was on for young and old, left and right, centre-left and centre-right, green and red — all the political hues and alliances that make up the colourful custard of Italian politics. Cacciari's chief opponent Giancarlo Galan — who just happens to be another equally ambitious local pollie whom he is trying to unseat as President of the much larger and more influential regional government of Veneto — accused the former mayor of being 'ready to sacrifice even the saving of Venice to his electoral campaign'. Enter Moses. 'We want the Moses dykes,' Galan said, 'while the mayor suggests that citizens resolve the water problem by wearing boots.' According to Christopher Emsden in the *Italy Daily*, Galan was poking fun at the Cacciari administration's decision the week before to set up a call centre 'allowing residents to be warned of high tide days before venturing out onto the sidewalks'.

'Hitching one's electoral campaign to the dyke project,' wrote Emsden, 'could backfire.' Meanwhile, the unresolved problem of securing a safe, 'watertight' future for Venice remains unresolved. According to marine engineer Luigi Torretti, head of a consortium that has been dredging and cleaning the city's canals and raising its footpaths in an attempt to combat the high tides and corrosion, 'the big solution — whatever it is — will not solve all the city's problems. I agree that we need to do something big to stop the sea, but we should be sure that Moses is the right solution before the state spends 5 trillion lire on a project that will take ten years to complete.' A decent pot of lire.

But do the Venetians, indeed, the Italians, really have a choice? What price history? What price art? What price Venice? Probably more than anyone else, they should know the answer to these imponderables.

Whatever happened to the international 'Save Venice' campaign that was floated, no pun intended, some years back? Is Venice Italy's problem, or a problem for us all, we who claim we want to preserve the best of our cultural past while we're charging headlong into the worst of our technological future?

Changing as Fast as Italy Changes Governments

There are some places, we're told, where time stands still. That's clearly true of Venice. But more to the point, in Venice, time is of little significance or consequence. It is not a case of when you're there or for how long, but rather where you are. In that winter of 1999, neither the city nor its carnival were 'feasts lost in the mists of time', as the official visitors' brochure put it. For better or worse, they are in the here and now. I only had to look around me. Venice was the same Venice, but it wasn't.

Making its way down the still-magnificent expanse of the Grand Canal, a yellow Volkswagen Beetle on a promotional barge didn't look right in its ageless vehicle-free surroundings.

But, in 1999, the Venice Carnevale was marketed, sponsored, and brought to the world by Volkswagen.

Venice exemplifies the Italian contradiction. Regarded by so many as the most amazing city in the world, it remains incredibly alluring. But at the same time, it is repelling Venetians. Mass tourism and exorbitant house prices have driven the majority of Venetians back over the water to Mestre.

Over the past thirty to forty years, the permanent Venetian population has slumped from around a quarter of a million to something like 50 000 or 60 000 today. At night, Venice is as deserted as a ghost town, its handful of hardy, full-time residents reduced to prisoners in the most beautiful city on Earth, itself rapidly becoming a theme park for tourists. 'Those of us who are left,' one young couple told Matt Frei, 'will probably be made to wear traditional Venetian costumes. For us, life will become one long historical pageant.'

Why do I not feel much sympathy for their plight? It could be a hell of a lot worse. Venice could go right under when the next tide or flood rushes into the Piazza San Marco and they could end up very wet, drowned, or, God forbid, living across the causeway among the slag-heaps and refineries. Quite frankly, I can think of far worse places to live.

Every time I have got off the *vaporetto*, climbed the low steps, boarded one of Italy's perpetually punctual *treni* at the always boisterous and crowded Stazione Santa Lucia, settled into my compartment and left that liquid wonderland, I have never once felt that I wouldn't be back — if it's still there, of course, the next time I can make it! I do hope that my kids' kids get to marvel at Venice — like Kirsty and I and our kids have. If Venice survives the next two generations (or even more), it will be the result of a wild paradigm swing in international values, a swing, in non-ideological terms, in the 'right' direction.

In the meantime, although it's in grave danger of becoming the world's most expensive and sophisticated theme park, Venice makes a mockery of so-called 'progress'. As a place of human habitation, it hasn't progressed, it's probably regressed, at least in the structural sense. The paradox on this occasion is that the more Venice regresses, the more popular it becomes. If we were to ponder that miraculous contradiction as much as we ponder the vagaries of the microchip, maybe we would find ourselves getting a little closer to a definition of genuine human advancement.

David *Contro* Gabriel

This may sound like crass cultural sacrilege, but up until quite recently in Florence, if Michelangelo were to find himself working on a sculpture to please the masses, he would probably not choose David as his subject, he would almost certainly choose Gabriel. To confuse things further, this latter-day *Fiorentino* icon was not even an archangel. He was a post-modern Gabriel, one with no apparent religious significance in the normal sense.

Indeed, he was an overtly temporal, extremely physical being, but nevertheless one with a set of almost religious, even cultish, followers. Indeed, his most devoted admirers believed he had wings like his religious namesake. It was true that, on occasions, this special being reached such ethereal heights in his chosen earthly task that this fantasy became almost real.

I speak of Gabriel Omar Batistuta, formerly of Fiorentina but now with AS Roma, a mere footballer, a soccer player, a *calciatore*, if indeed there is such a thing as a 'mere footballer'. In a nation where there are two acknowledged religions, Catholicism and *calcio*, where intensity of faith and belief are concerned about the only difference between the two is that one starts with a capital letter and the other doesn't.

The connection between *calcio* and the soul of contemporary Italy is inextricable. Indeed, *calcio* is intrinsically cultural, inherently cultural, essentially cultural — provided that that culture is 'national, enlightening, refining and edifying', as any half-decent thesaurus will tell you.

Batistuta is one of the world's most sought after and highly paid soccer players. He is a combination of sporting hero, rock star and, in the Mediterranean context, for better or worse, Spanish matador. While foreign tourists queued for hours to see the great works at the Uffizi and the original

David at the Galleria Della Academia, Italians queued to see 'the Argentino' weave his very different magic, regarded by many — and not just football fanatics, of whom there are plenty — as being its own art form. The powerful goals he scored for Fiorentina with almost monotonous regularity coined their very own word. Until he moved to Rome, 'Batigol!' became a normal part of the everyday Florentine lexicon.

Most days, after morning and afternoon *allenamento*, training, Batistuta dined well but inconspicuously in the same tastefully unpretentious but proud trattoria a few hundred metres from the River Arno, just south of the Ponte Vecchio. The thousands of gullible Japanese, American and other tourists shopping at the famous medieval bridge's gold and silver shops were probably unaware of Batistuta's 'David' status. But if they had stayed longer in one place than your average tourist seems inclined to do, they would have. While it lasted, the Batistuta phenomenon pervaded Florentine social life. Batistuta was not just a talented *giocatore*, not just one of soccer's superstars. The Reebok-sponsored multimillionaire footballer was also a product, a marketing vehicle, a commercial profit-maker for himself and for the umpteen corporations and entrepreneurs who sought him out.

For example, towards the end of the 1998–1999 *stagione di calcio*, football season, a new perfume, Essenza di Campione, propelled its way onto the already crowded

European cosmetics market in a blaze of *pubblicità*, with Batistuta's ruggedly handsome Latin looks as its marketing hook. The man himself, with his long brown tresses, amazing physique and boyish but craggy aquiline features, fancied himself as the embodiment of a North American Indian chieftain. He extolled the Cheyenne qualities of bravery, leadership, affinity with the wind, the sun, earth, water and fire and the natural strength and wisdom they have always appeared to carry. Clearly here was someone smarter than your average football star.

Florence and Football — A Contradiction in Cultural Terms?

These days, of course, Florentines don't have Michelangelo, nor do they have Batistuta. He defected to Fiorentina's hated rivals from the south, AS Roma, at the end of the 1999–2000 season for a reported transfer fee of US$33 million and an annual salary of US$5.2 million, making him the highest paid player in the history of Italian soccer.

But back in 1999, the Argentinian was still with Fiorentina's 'Viola' and one afternoon I managed to catch a particularly hard-fought *partita di calcio* in which Fiorentina triumphed, ironically, over Batistuta's future club. After it was over, Mary McCarthy's *The Stones of Florence* was a pleasant enough way to while away the hour-long train journey from Florence's Stazione Santa Maria Novella to San Giovanni Valdarno. In Italy, enjoying a piece of literature on the way home from a football match is not necessarily a contradiction in cultural terms — and if it is, so what? Look again at your definition of culture, not what the dictionaries say it is, but what it really is — the things other than the menial mundanities of the daily grind that make people feel momentarily better about the menial and the mundane. *Calcio* does that. Gabriel Batistuta does that.

McCarthy, of course, got herself quite a reputation via her steamy 1970s novel *The Group*, one of those books that seemed for some inexplicable reason to invariably 'fall open' at particular pages. But *The Stones of Florence* is more chaste than cheeky, more sumptuous than sensuous, more telling than titillating, although anyone reading it who had not enjoyed the splendour of the northern Italian 'city of light' would definitely be tempted by both its temporal and non-temporal attributes.

McCarthy asserts that the Florentines invented the Renaissance, hence the modern world. But McCarthy had a feeling that at some point — maybe between Giotto and Michelangelo — a terrible mistake was committed in Florence, a mistake to do with 'power and megalomania, or gigantism of the human ego'. David was said to have a 'cold, vain stare in love with his own strength and beauty'. And this, a comment that's been ringing in the head of this political animal ever since that day on the regional 7.18 from Florence to San Giovanni Valdarno: 'This feeling that Florence was the scene of the original crime or error was hard to avoid just after the last World War, when power and technology had reduced so much to rubble.'

Power and technology reducing so much to rubble? In Italy, you can go to a football match and come away with much more than a good or a bad result. I turned to my newspaper and to the *calcio* results for the rest of the country. The Italian therapy was working.

Walk, Don't Run, on the Stones of Florence

In Florence you wander aimlessly yet with an aim — which sounds ridiculous unless you've actually been a Florentine wanderer. We're always being told that there are places all around the world, usually cities or towns, where the only way to get a sense of and feeling for that particular place is to walk. But wandering is very different from walking. To walk, you look at a map, work out a few carefully chosen directions and destinations and head off knowing, at least according to the map, where you are going and maybe even why. But walking, you might not get to see what you *came* to see because you're far too busy with your head in your map. You're usually so hellbent on making sure you haven't missed what you set out to see that you don't realise until it's too late that you already have. That doesn't happen when you're wandering. If you don't know what you're looking for, you're less likely to miss it. Stumbling unexpectedly out of a narrow flagstone lane in Florence's *centro* into the sumptuously open Piazza della Repubblica with its medieval arches and pillars is somehow a far sight better than knowing where it is and going directly to it. By the same token, each time you rediscover, more or less by chance, that the Piazza della Signoria signposting that the Uffizzi Galeria is only a few excited steps away, it always feels like the first time. There's always a new or different *portico* hiding yet another secret *giardino* or tiled *terrazzo* or even a locals' bar whose *caffè macchiato* you haven't tried.

But most tourists and travellers to Florence — and they've been pouring into that incredible place in their millions for centuries — make it in and out of the city without even knowing that it is yet another soccer-mad Italian city. In much the same way but on a totally different tack, they usually experience little if anything of its contemporary politics. Why, by and large, do guidebooks, jam-packed as they are with other both useful and useless information, persist in avoiding politics? Are they hoping against hope that if we don't mention it, it might go away?

Maybe if they did mention basic politics or at least an overview of them, it might make their readers' destinations even more interesting than they already hope they will be.

It could also mean that many of the nuances and subtleties of life in the host country might make more sense than they do when a visitor has no idea where the locals are coming from in terms of their value judgments. Let's not kid ourselves that fundamental values and ideological perspectives — or, in some cases, the lack of them — do not affect how people live, love, work and play. The Italians, in wondrous Florence or anywhere else, engage in all four of these essential life activities with passion and aggression. Rightly or wrongly, they also appear to believe that the politics of the place and time affect how they go about these activities.

To the Italians and, as a general rule, Europeans, politics mean a hell of a lot more than how much tax they pay or whether interest rates are going up or down. Unfortunately, the same can't be said of other parts of the world, including one you may be familiar with south of Papua New Guinea and west of New Zealand.

Phoney Fascism on the Footy Field

To be honest, there was the odd moment or two during the twelve-month evolution of this concept of an Italy dominated by football, food and politics when I began to think that maybe I was pushing the association a little far, possibly even giving it a significance it didn't quite deserve. But as often as these doubts cropped up, there was yet another illustration of its pertinency. This happened on near enough to a daily basis to make *calcio* a running political issue in and of itself. Some instances were trivial, like MPs voting not to sit in Parliament for fear of not being able to attend matches involving teams they supported. But others had a distinctly ideological import to them. Some were lighthearted enough to be dismissible, but even those could still take on a political dimension.

A case in point was the antics, early in the 1999–2000 season, of Gianluigi Buffon, the *portiere*, goalkeeper, for both the popular Parma club in Serie A and the Italian national team. Buffon is a genuine star of the game and certainly no 'buffoon'. But following what he intended to be nothing more than a well-intentioned onfield gesture, Buffon suddenly found himself in political hot water. After some pretty ordinary performances and some equally unimpressive results by his Parma side, the brilliant but easygoing keeper took it upon himself to try and lift both the spirits and the standard of play of his blue-and-yellow-shirted teammates. As Buffon saw things from his vantage point between the goalposts, the team had been throwing away too many matches it should have won. To make his point, Buffon scribbled a cryptic message on his jersey, 'Boia chi molla!', a motto-like phrase which loosely translates as 'Damn those who give up!' It was not an unreasonable sentiment for a team of such flagging fortunes. But unfortunately for Buffon, there was a political catch.

'Boia chi molla!', it was revealed, was an old Fascist slogan from the days of 'Il Duce', Benito Mussolini. Within twenty-four hours, Buffon's genuinely innocent stunt had turned into a political bombshell with headlines to match. Before he could muster even a word in his defence, Alessandra Mussolini, Il Duce's glamorous and controversial granddaughter, a far right MP and a young woman who seldom misses an opportunity for self-promotion, jumped on the Buffon bandwagon — and all over her left-wing opponents.

The then centre-left government of former Communist Massimo D'Alema went off its anti-fascist face. Interior Minister Rosa Russo Jervolino threw political caution to the wind and lambasted the guileless national hero, Buffon, for displaying poor political taste.

The redoubtable Ms Mussolini — not the most unattractive or modest politician to grace the benches of any parliament — flashed a 'Boia Chi Molla!' T-shirt in the Parliament. Classically Italian parliamentary chaos ensued. In the melee and name-calling that followed, the legislative session had to be suspended, not once but twice, as MPs from the other side of the ideological divide screamed at the smiling, red-lipped granddaughter of Il Duce to cover up the 'offending phrase' or get out of the chamber. Mussolini refused. She protested that there was nothing wrong with her or, by inference, Italy's national goalkeeper displaying an old Fascist slogan. She had managed to turn Buffon's naïve stunt on the football field into a heated Left-Right debate on the very nature of parliamentary democracy itself.

'For 280 days out of 365, we have to see red banners and Che Guevara posters on State television,' Mussolini shouted back at her politically 'pink' adversaries. 'It's unacceptable that some symbols are deemed all right and others are not.' It was on that politically provocative note that, unblushing, she employed a more obvious sort of provocation. With more than a touch of her acknowledged post-feminist guile, she removed her sweater. One outraged government MP demanded that the Speaker of the House order her to put the sweater back on. Others, for unreported reasons, did not. The demand to 'put it back on' was not without its degree of irony. Back in 1983, in pre-political life, a pouting Mussolini had posed for *Playboy* magazine. A few years later — either for the art, the money or, in more ways than one, the exposure — she did the same for a German soft-porn weekly. As Matt Frei has commented: 'All of this is potentially embarrassing. Oddly enough, it [Mussolini's nude photographic cavorting] was never used by the opposition — perhaps because the pictures would have boosted her support.'

Gabrielle Kahn, a staff writer with the *Italy Daily*, pointed out after the Buffon incident and the parliamentary ruckus that followed that the serious accusation levelled against Mussolini was that she was 'contributing to the climate of hooliganism in the national soccer stadiums'. Football violence has always been a vexed issue that only adds to the potent brew of Italian football and Italian politics. Even so, the Fascists, reconstructed and non-reconstructed Communists, Socialists, Christian Democrats, the Northern League — in fact the entire *mistura di politica* inhabiting Italy's political circus — all had a great day in the National Parliament near the Piazza Colonna in Rome.

Back in Parma, home of the ubiquitous Italian cheese we are all obliged to grate on our *spaghetti con ragù*, the crestfallen Gianluigi Buffon was collecting his thoughts and his shattered good intentions. The young goalkeeping prodigy was bemused by all the fuss. Accepting that he'd made a mistake, albeit an innocent one, an apologetic Buffon told the local media that he hadn't bargained for the political carry-on. 'I don't know anything about politics,' he said in an almost un-Italian admission. 'I didn't know that it was a right-wing slogan.' He reiterated that his sole intention had been to stir his teammates on to greater heights, 'to inspire them', as he put it. Basically, what he was trying to say was 'For God's sake, guys, get your finger out!' or 'How about a bit more effort, fellas?' or 'Come on! Don't throw in the towel just yet!'

As things calmed down after the initial rumpus, parliamentary chaos and media uproar, to become merely a controversial political issue, Buffon, the reluctant political activist, had this cogent comment: 'After having seen the images of what happened in Parliament, I believe that compared to that, what I did was nothing!'

How Much is Too Much?

In recent times, particularly the last couple of years, professional sport, especially football, has edged closer to pure entertainment. Commensurate with this has been the shift in players' remuneration. The amounts are almost impossible to justify. Not only old-fashioned Marxists, monetary bigots and ordinary old bearers of envy and jealousy are upset and concerned. Equity and fairness do not apply in this climate of inflated salaries and transfer fees and, not without reason, many of the punters, the paying public, are beginning to jump up and down about it.

Italy is a classic example. Player payments have become more than just a financial issue. It has swollen into a politico-economic debate. You could go so far as to say it has become an ideological, even moral controversy, a question of basic human ethics. But then again, these days, where does professional sport end and mass commercial entertainment begin? The fact is there is no dividing line anymore — whether we like it or not.

In their own laissez-faire fashion, the Italians are onto the problem. Well, they *know* there is a problem. But the more they talk and argue about it, the higher the players' payments seem to go. Maybe they believe that it will all sort itself out. That's their normal attitude to the things they take far less seriously than their football.

During the two European football seasons that ran their course during our year in Italy, probably the most potent argument on this whole issue of football, money, power and arrogance came not just from Italy — where the polemic had already been raging in bars and on stadium terraces on a daily basis for years — but other European countries, including that other hot-blooded, roundball-mad Latin-Mediterranean land, Spain.

Rayo Vallecano is a team from Vallecas, a working-class neighbourhood in the generally swinging Spanish capital, Madrid. For a while there, the 'Vallecas Thunderbolts', as the locals affectionately dub their favourites, bobbed up to give a whole new sporting definition to the well-worn rags-to-riches maxim.

Although they have made it into the coveted Spanish First Division, the Primera Liga, Rayo doesn't have its own practice pitch, has no training gym, has a woman for President, unusual to say the least in España, one of the world's bastions of machismo, and makes do on a near-subsistence budget in an era of multimillion-dollar club turnovers. On top of all this, somehow or other, they have scored an American, of all nationalities, as their goalkeeper — a bit like the New York Giants having a Thai pitcher!

John Vinocur of the *International Herald Tribune* described Rayo as 'a corner store grocery in the world of Big Soccer'. However, promoted to the top flight for the 1999–2000 season, lowly Rayo took everyone by complete surprise in the opening rounds of the competition by leaping miraculously to the top of the ladder, well ahead of the likes of immensely rich and powerful crosstown rivals Real Madrid.

Rayo found themselves on an amazing winning streak, despite having no website, no money to buy star players, an annual budget about a tenth of Real Madrid's, a meagre fifteen full-time employees and less than 6000 paid-up season ticket-holders. Along with Barcelona, that other giant of Spanish football, Real has a whopping 100000 *socios*, or paying supporters. But three weeks into the Spanish championship, Rayo had beaten heavyweights Atletico Madrid and Celta Vigo and were unlucky to lose to highly rated Real Zaragoza. Despite these outstanding early season wins, Rayo's admirably modest ambitions were to remain high enough up the premiership ladder to stay in the Spanish First Division.

How long did this footballing 'Cinderella story' last? In 1999–2000 Rayo finished respectably mid-table in ninth position, and, more importantly, qualified for the UEFA Cup.

So what has this rags-to-riches story from Spain to do with the mounting international row over how much sportsmen and woman should get paid, let alone the relationship between soccer and politics? Well, a lot really. To explain, it's necessary to take a look at another curious football-money tale, the quite sad saga surrounding the 1999 summer transfer of the brilliant but erratic young Afro-French striker, Nicolas Anelka. Anelka was bought from leading English club Arsenal by Real Madrid. They paid a mere US$36 million!

During the period when Rayo was confounding the experts and topping the Liga, the enormously expensive Anelka, after weeks of frighteningly immature will-he-or-won't-he indecision before finally making the move to Real, was failing to live up to both the giant Madrid club's expectations and his extravagant transfer fee. In fact, while Rayo's minnows were lifting their game and themselves to the top of the table, the controversial Anelka was not even getting his name on the scoresheet. In fact, he wasn't even staying on the field for the full ninety minutes.

The highly regarded Javier Clemente, a former coach of the Spanish national XI, went further than most, calling Anelka's price tag an insult to Spanish society. 'In a modest country with a lot of cultural, social and political deficiencies, those millions could do a lot,' he said. 'I think Madrid has enough social problems so that modest people are not asking themselves, above all, if Anelka is going to score twenty-five goals. With these millions, you could take care of everybody who's hungry in Madrid.'

'The image leaves a lasting impression. In a Reuters photograph, a boy maybe three years of age is rapt in child's play. Elegantly balanced, eyes on the ball, his right foot kicking it; this is the figure of the innocence and sheer fun of soccer. In the background is a jumble of belongings in a Turkish tented camp days after the devastating earthquake. The infant's ability to find distraction in a ball is a reminder of what power, what joy the game holds — for children of all ages. It might also temper the hype, the cant, the nationalism aroused by the same game.'

So wrote unapologetic football nut Rob Hughes, chief sportswriter for *The Times* of London. Along with the hype, the cant and the nationalism, Hughes could also have tossed in the increasing moneymania I've been referring to. But his lyrical reflections on the young Turkish earthquake survivor make a sober point about the worldwide power of football.

Between August and September 1999, a monster 7.4 earthquake in northwestern Turkey took 15 000 lives. Then, a very short time later, another killer quake of less devastating magnitude — 5.9 — ripped through the northern suburbs of the Greek capital Athens taking, fortunately, far fewer lives. At the same time, forty-four nations were competing in the final qualification rounds of the Euro 2000 football tournament. All forty-four, of course, including Turkey and Greece, still reeling from the quakes, aspired to make the finals.

The previous October, the proud red-and-white-shirted Turks, their strips adorned with Islamic crescents, had, against the odds and the run of play, beaten the mighty Germans. They had been performing well enough since then to be rated a good chance to make the final cut for Euro 2000.

Immediately after the 1999 quake, they travelled to Belfast and beat the formidable Northern Ireland 3–0.

'Reports out of the earthquake zone suggested that survivors — even those grieving — rejoiced at the victory,' Hughes wrote. 'Pride one can understand, but those reports spoke of some spiritual uplift, a sense of defiance and renewal from such a trivial event as a soccer match. From the safe land on which I stand, that appears to invest too much in a sport, too great a burden on mere players.'

Maybe, maybe not. Hughes also was quick to remind readers that the little bloke who survived the quake to kick a ball around his new tent home probably didn't even have a television to see the Turkish national side's games. 'He might be too young to concern himself with grown-up hang-ups about something he finds so sweet and so engrossing.'

Clearly stirred by the sight of the kid, Hughes, like others before him, was moved to have a go at the exorbitantly paid Nicolas Anelka. 'Poor, poor Anelka! He couldn't play in London,' he said, 'because the press bothered him. He can't stand the media circus in Madrid either following his US$36 million move; they depress him by putting his picture in the papers!'

After an apparently very ordinary display for his French national team the week before, Anelka had threatened to quit the game altogether — at the ripe old age of twenty. 'Take a look, Nicolas, at the boy from Turkey,' Hughes fumed. 'See that it is a gift, a joy, an escape from the truly depressing side of life to be blessed with talent some people pay millions for. One day, perhaps, the boy [in the Reuters photo] will aspire to exchange his innocent expression for a pay cheque. All we can hope is that he does not grow so full of his own self-importance that he loses the beauty of playing.'

Sometimes, I thought, it's not so bad to identify with journalists. Some, not many of them, can actually manage to be human beings first and media machines later.

In the same month that the front page of the *International Herald Tribune* tipped me off to the delightful story about the 'Vallecas Thunderbolts', another story, related more to the millions who cannot tell a rags-to-riches tale, was buried in the op-ed pages. I saw and heard it nowhere else.

This is how David Nyhan of the *Boston Globe* summed up the scant coverage of world poverty: 'Human nature being what it is, the hawkers of news prosper more off what arouses the customer than what accurately informs.' Pictures of kids being dragged miraculously from a post-earthquake rubble or an Indonesian riot squad in full flight are 'more compelling than footage of some middle-aged bureaucrat rattling on about poverty'. Unfortunately, Nyhan is correct. However, I don't know that the cause is 'human nature' — whatever that is and if indeed it even exists. Try rank stupidity, counter-productive egocentricity or even media myopia as more valid explanations. These are much closer to the mark than 'human nature' — something we claim we cannot change but which we regularly blame for all that's ill and evil in the world.

The 'middle-aged bureaucrat' Nyhan was referring to was, in fact, James Wolfensohn, an expat Australian. Wolfensohn is the head of the World Bank. The truth is that Wolfensohn, a lawyer and highly successful merchant banker in another life, has far more to contribute to the international debate on poverty than mere bureaucratic prattle.

Having interviewed him a few years back, politically he's difficult to pin down, but he carries with him a consciousness of the needs of a civil society and a humane world. A highly intelligent, aware, charming sort of bloke, for years Wolfensohn aggressively sought the prestigious but close-to-thankless World Bank job. Some even claim he openly lobbied Democrat President Jimmy Carter and later the Clintons to get it. Since he landed the plum role — whatever his motivation, altruistic or otherwise — he's spent his time in the post beating the world poverty drum at every opportunity. Unlike many with a blind eye, he's obviously convinced it is a problem and should be a priority for both governments and business throughout the world.

Speaking before the 1999 annual meeting of the World Bank and the International Monetary Fund (IMF) in Washington, Wolfensohn sent off some explosive statistical ICBMs. They are easier to take in if listed.

- Per capita, future incomes throughout the world will stagnate or decline in all regions except East and South-East Asia — probably because in those two economically battered regions they have nowhere to go but up after the so-called Asian financial meltdown.

- Some 1.5 billion of the world's 5 billion-plus population — to all intents and purposes, more than one in four human beings — are still lacking access to safe water.

- Close to 125 million children do not receive even a primary school education. Despite the much-vaunted Internet, as Wolfensohn pointed out, we live in 'a world where the information gap is widening'.

- The world's forests 'are being destroyed at the rate of an acre a second'.

- Half the world's population gets by on the contemptible equivalent of $2 dollars a day or even less. Astonishingly, half that number actually lives on less than a dollar a day.

- When a child born in 2000 reaches the age of twenty-five in 2025, there will be another two billion people on the planet, making a total of eight billion, all of them 'fighting for air, water, food, space, roofs, jobs, schooling, roads, sewers, farmland'. Only development will spare them a life of what Wolfensohn describes as 'perilous poverty'.

Wolfensohn, the harbinger of this statistical gloom and doom, has been described as the individual 'more responsible than any other, perhaps even more than the President of the United States, for the wellbeing of mankind and the development of economic structures to make its futures more secure'. The crux of Wolfensohn's address to the annual meeting in Washington was that all the development and growth in the world in recent decades has not been enough — or perhaps not the right kind — to ensure the reduction, let alone the elimination, of global poverty. This surely means that we're still getting things horribly wrong. 'In other words,' Wolfensohn said, 'if as a race we are serious about reducing the persistent and worsening poverty levels plaguing peoples on board Spaceship Earth, we have been doing nowhere near enough. Poverty is much more than a matter of income alone. The poor seek a sense of wellbeing — which is peace of mind.'

Wolfensohn quoted from a revealing World Bank study, 'Voices of the Poor', distilled from the comments of 60 000 identifiably poor individuals from sixty different countries. What do they themselves say about being poor? What do they want from the not-so-poor, from governments, from corporations, even from charities and aid agencies? 'It is good health, community and safety. It is choice and freedom as well as a steady source of income,' said one. 'To live in love without hunger,' said another, an old woman from famine-riven Africa. 'To be well is to know what will happen to me tomorrow,' answered a survivor of Eastern European communism, now caught between a discredited system he doesn't want and a new one he was promised but doesn't have.

What thinnest-edge-of-the-wedge links the head of the World Bank's concerns about global poverty with the game of football? Frankly, football is about the only pleasure many of the world's very poorest people have. Soccer crosses all barriers.

The Fever You Have to Have!

In Italy — indeed, throughout the entire continent of Europe, rich or poor — you can pretend not to be interested in football, but you can never ignore it. No matter how hard the anti-football minority might try to minimise its influence, it is everywhere. In every city, town, village, avenue, street, back lane, vacant allotment, patch of dirt, park, schoolyard, classroom, office block, shop, living room, even church, nothing, nowhere and no one escapes *calcio*. 'Every Sunday afternoon during the season,' wrote Charles Richards in *The New Italians*, 'you see couples sitting at café tables, a small transistor between them, or a father out with his family for a stroll, a radio pressed to his ear listening to live coverage of the local game.' Richards makes an useful point about *calcio*'s incursion into daily Italian life, borne out by personal experience of the pompous anti-football types who rush to declare their disdain for the roundball phenomenon, yet as Richards says, are 'well-informed about the sport'.

Yes, soccer is a sport. But it is also a pillar of European society, exemplified by the near-religious status it takes on in Italy. Silvio Berlusconi calls it 'the modern equivalent of bread and circuses'. David Dale, an Australian writer I know and whom I always presumed was not exactly a sports-freak, even included soccer as No. 28 in his book *100 Things Everyone Needs to Know About Italy*. In its current form, David writes, soccer was introduced into Italy in the late 1800s when the English factory owners of Genoa, Turin and Milan 'set up teams to keep their workers fit'. 'It spread like typhoid,' he wrote, 'and nowadays *il calcio* is more powerful than a religion.' As he observed, on any Sunday between September and June, when the Italian finals are played, 'most people don't go to church, but they tune into television or to a radio if they're out in a café, to learn how their local team is going. Then they spend most of their Mondays conducting post-mortems on the game.'

In a serious sociological way, to be anti-football is to be anti-Italian. Soccer fever is virulent in Italy. But it's a fever you have to have if you're Italian. You can't build up any real resistance to it. Every season — rain, hail or shine — you know you're going to get it. And when you do get it, you can't shake it off. A couple of days in bed won't cure it. It's there on the telly almost every day and night. And, while we're on the subject, the typhoid connection is not coincidental. Writer Paul Hofmann has explained it simply for the non-medically-minded: 'The Italian idiom likens the excitement caused by spectator sports to the fever produced by typhus, calling it *tifo*.' The Italian soccer fan, a word that in itself has the same etymology as the far less benign 'fanatic', is known as a *tifoso*, a typhus patient!

David Dale also makes the point, as others have, about the binding power of soccer. As he says, winning the World Cup in 1982 not only sent the Italians into a frenzy, 'it finally united twenty regions which, until then, had barely acknowledged that they were part of the one country.' But so too did the collective shout of agony when Roby Baggio failed to slot the vital penalty at USA '94. 'Baggio has never really recovered from his 1994 World Cup embarrassment,' noted Dale. 'When it comes to *calcio*, Italians hold long grudges.'

God's Game — Or Mammon's?

The unavoidable presence of *calcio* in Italian and European life was best summed up by an April 1999 *Italy Daily* headline: 'Lazio's Performance Cheers Investors and Fans Alike'.

A year earlier, Lazio, one of the country's richest and most glamorous clubs, had become the first Italian soccer club to be listed on the stockmarket. Shares in the club rose more than 260 per cent, compared to a miserly 6 per cent over the same period for Italy's official blue-chip index. The surge was particularly strong during the third week of February when Lazio powered into the competition lead for the first time in twenty-five years. Their performance was reason enough, it seems, for the club's supporters to go beyond yelling from the stands and actually hurl real money at the club. The Italian Stock Exchange was not too sure how to handle the 'irrational volatility' of a football-led boom in the market and suspended trading in Lazio stocks after they were bid up by almost 90 per cent, before the market opened on the Monday after a match. Over the next three trading days, Lazio shares increased in value by a further 95 per cent. When shares in Società Sportiva Lazio, the Lazio trading company, debuted on the Italian stock exchange at 5900 lire each, the team was in second place in Serie A and was set to play in a UEFA Cup match in Paris. Lazio shares soared by 12 per cent in anticipation of the match and trading had to be briefly suspended.

As it turned out, Lazio was beaten in Serie A by another similarly prestigious but unlisted Italian club, Inter Milan. The following day, both Lazio fans' enthusiasm for the team and the price of the club's shares took a dive. At the completion of the 1998 season, Lazio finished a very ordinary seventh. A few months later the share price fell to an all-time low of 3705 lire. However, at the end of the first year of trading, shares were worth a massive 14 675 lire!

For those not aware of soccer's enormous commercial clout worldwide, there actually exists a specialised journal for the all-important London financial community called, predictably, *Soccer Investor*, a name that says it all. In the UK, more than twenty soccer clubs have gone public over the past fifteen years.

The incongruous yet exciting idea of sharetrading in an extravagantly popular sport with international corporate tentacles and ownership connections that read like a veritable 'Who's Who' of Italian business, was a bit beyond the regular risktakers, the traditional venture capitalists of the market. They were far more used to trading in zillions of lire, pounds, marks, francs, yen and dollars to buy and sell everything from water to nuclear waste. But when it came to trading in something as popular, harmless and unpredictable as twenty-two talented and superbly fit young men entertaining hundreds of thousands of fans each weekend by kicking a round leather ball around a flat, grassy rectangle, they were nowhere near as daring or confident.

It was clear that football share prices responded more to success on the field than to any financial statement. In 1998, Lazio shares were again suspended after they thrashed lowly Udinese 3–0 a day earlier. But for whatever reason, they went up again a couple of days later by another 10 per cent, and there had not even been a match in between. In this sort of unpredictable climate, even besotted Lazio fans became wary of the market's fluctuations.

Marco Rola, a Roman accountant who you would think would understand the vagaries of the market better than most, told the local media that like hundreds of other 'Lazio maniacs', he had intended holding on to his prized shares in the club forever. But their ups and downs bothered him. 'I didn't want to face the dilemma of being both a fan of the team but peeved by the performance of the stock,' he said.

Probably only a football fan of the intense Italian variety could find his or herself with a cash-versus-commitment dilemma — not the sort of thing that normally drives stock up or down!

Late in the 1999 season, Lazio's fortunes on the field were still affecting the financial fortunes of its market-oriented supporters. Fluctuations were occurring on a match-by-match basis. In one instance, fans, disgruntled after Lazio had drawn a vital game against high-flying Fiorentina, a draw that forced them down into second place in Serie A with only one match to play, unloaded their shares post-haste. The club actually suffered what the market terms 'a theoretical drop' of close to 70 per cent. As a result, it was suspended on the country's stock exchange, Milan. But even then, the market's connection to the sport was evident. An Italian finance writer reported that Società Sportiva Lazio had shed a mere 40 billion lire of market capitalisation — less than the transfer fee Lazio paid Atletico Madrid the previous summer for star striker Christian Vieri.

Lazio's chairman, Sergio Cragnotti, is also the boss of the monstrously sized Cirio food company, the club's naming rights sponsor. Lazio rival Fiorentina, which was leading Serie A until overtaken by the listed Roman club, is in itself a further example of the symbiotic relationship of Italian football, Italian finance, and even Italian politics. Vittorio Cecchi Gori, the owner of Fiorentina, also owns TeleMontecarlo, a pay-TV conglomerate. His brother is a senator in Italy's Upper House. However, Cecchi Gori is not as certain as Cragnotti that publicly listing is the way to go. 'It puts fans at risk,' he said at the height of Lazio's market fluctuations. According to Christopher Emsden, Cecchi Gori prefers to issue Fiorentina bonds, allowing the team's fans to 'be tapped to subsidise what amounts to a low-interest loan for the club'. While Lazio was trading on the stock exchange, Cecchi Gori arranged a 60 billion lire (near enough to US$26 million) bond offer underwritten by US multinational finance company Merrill Lynch. The offer paid 4.75 per cent interest and, significantly, as Emsden noted, costs Fiorentina much less than a bank loan.

Many other Italian soccer clubs have been toying with the idea of floating themselves. But, by and large, Italian investors remain nervous, maybe because the heavily backed Lazio club has suffered billion-lire losses despite hikes in revenue. One problem is that much of the revenue is spent on buying new players in a vastly inflated transfer market. Lazio, one of the few Italian clubs to make money in the

1998 season, was a prime example, immediately going on a wild spending spree to beef up its squad with huge and expensive stars like Christian Vieri and Chilean Marcelo Salas. The player market is so volatile that one Italian magazine noted very seriously that Lazio would be financially better off if it lost the title. Apart from anything else, the 13 billion lire prize would have to be shared with the players of the winning team. The 7 billion lire second prize, on the other hand, was theirs to keep.

The role of players, off as well as on the field, has become critical. When Lazio's shares rocketed early in the 1999 season, stock analysts and brokers actually attributed the surge, at least in part, to an injury sustained in a match the weekend before by Gabriel Batistuta, then Fiorentina's *capitano* and goal-a-game sharpshooter. When Batistuta missed six games, Fiorentina lost the Serie A top spot, and Lazio took over the top spot in Serie A, its stocks off the field soared! But when it comes to business-cum-soccer's growing pains over player payments, the Christian Vieri story has it all.

When Lazio spent US$28 million to lure the star striker back to his homeland from Spain, then the third highest transfer fee in soccer's history, he was part of a multibillion lire outlay that also included the signatures of other stars from Chile, Spain and Yugoslavia. But Vieri was the key. 'Vieri is important to us not only because he is a top striker, but because he is a tireless fighter,' Lazio's then manager-coach, Sven-Goran Eriksson, said of the then twenty-five-year-old Italian-born, Australian-raised player: 'He exhausts his opponents for the entire ninety minutes and also manages to be lethal, both with his head and with his left foot. I am not sure that Lazio would be where it is now if we didn't have Vieri.' Of course, since then both Vieri and Eriksson have left the club — Eriksson to coach England — yet the purchase of Vieri proved a boon to the club on a number of fronts.

When Lazio announced it had signed Vieri, Italy's top goalscorer in the previous summer's World Cup, its shares shot up 10 per cent, Italian journalist Nicholas Rigillo reported. 'Fan-investors paid no heed to his whopping transfer fee, even though investors warned that the soccer market was immature,' he wrote in the *Italy Daily*. Nevertheless, as one prominent stockbroker from Turin commented at the time: 'It is absolutely impossible to evaluate the consistency of a team's assets.' After all, he noted, a player, any soccer player, can easily break a leg and where does that leave the investment? And it doesn't have to be a broken leg. Even a simple head cold could dampen market enthusiasm.

For instance, while still with Lazio, Vieri was in Birmingham playing against Spanish side Mallorca. Early in the match, after scoring the opening goal, the tall, no-holds-barred *attaccante* was involved in a nasty head clash with an equally committed opposing *difensore*. Vieri came out of the exchange bleeding badly from the forehead and had to be heavily bandaged so he could complete the game. He did manage to go the distance and Lazio won the match, due in no small measure to the injured Vieri's valiant efforts. The win gave them the 1999 UEFA Cup Winners Cup.

But watching the television cutaways of Lazio's sartorially elegant executives — I hesitate to refer to them as mere football club officials — it was impossible to tell whether the concern they displayed was for Vieri's physical wellbeing, a jeopardised result, or their financial investment. To be fair — and given they were Italian — it was probably an intriguing mix of all three.

A week later, Vieri, the undisputed star of the Italian season, was back in the headlines. Again it was over money, more money than even *calcio*-crazy Italians could get their head around. Vieri was leaving Lazio for northerners Inter. It would be his sixth move in eight seasons, each time for an even sillier sum of money. He had been contracted to Lazio for five years at 7 billion lire a year, but Lazio president Cragnotti, a busy trader in his own club's shares, said Vieri might be allowed out of his multibillion-lira contract if 'an unreasonable offer' were made. Inter tabled a world-record offer of US$50 million. After the two-month summer break in football, a nothing period of the year which most Italians don't necessarily enjoy, in the long-awaited opening round match of the 1999–2000 season against Hellas Verona, Vieri scored a *tripletta*, three goals. His lethal left foot had done it again. It was not only a dream debut for his new club but an apparent vindication of the money invested in him by his new owners.

Given this almost miraculous, perfectly scripted start to the season by the world's then most expensive soccer player, the headlines predictably were over the top, many of them financial in their import. 'Inter's Dividend!' pronounced the *Italy Daily*. 'He cost an awful lot, but you just saw what we paid him for,' Inter's new coach Marcello Lippi beamed.

Meanwhile, by the end of the European and Italian seasons, both Lazio's fans and its investors — in some cases, one and the same — were obviously feeling more optimistic about the team and its stock, despite having lost Vieri, and were reassessing its market potential. Despite fluctuations in the stock as success on the pitch fluctuated, Società Sportiva Lazio finished the season as Italy's best-performing team and third-best performing stock. It was a successful marriage of football and finance.

The Biggest Single Product in the World

Television rights — both a seller's and a buyer's market where the world's most viewed sport, soccer, is concerned — is a huge influence, of course, on all this football-related financial activity. To its off-field players, it requires as much skill as anything going on in the stadia of Europe.

Four of Italy's leading clubs, Roma, Lazio, Fiorentina and Juventus, decided that on the TV rights front, unity was strength, agreeing to join forces in taking a 12 per cent stake in Stream, a pay-TV operation in which Rupert Murdoch's News Corporation controlled 35 per cent. Murdoch, not unlike Silvio Berlusconi, was superkeen to capitalise on the absurdly lucrative potential of soccer. At his News Corp AGM in New York in 1997, Murdoch, an Australian-born American citizen not known for being a particularly avid sports fan, went so far as to nominate soccer as 'the biggest single product in the world'. Quite a call. But if match and television audiences all over the world are any indication of soccer's money-making potential, this is no idle overstatement.

Surprisingly, though, the debate on why soccer-mad Italians should have to pay well in excess of 1 million lire annually, more than US$438, for a satellite dish and decoder to view matches played by their favourite Serie A teams has never really come to the boil. This is despite the fact that many Italians are sorely offended and disgruntled by the notion. But when people are in love, as they say, their reactions don't always make a lot of sense and blind, unqualified love is the only way to describe the way Italians feel about *calcio*.

However, the 'money game' is exceptional in its wacky contradictions. For every deal of Lazio and Murdoch proportions, there is an 'everyman' story going on somewhere in the boot, heel or toe of the Italian peninsula.

One such story came from Sardinia, the sun-blessed quasi-independent island bobbing about in the Mediterranean north-west of Rome. For a while in the late 1990s, Sardinia boasted a team, Cagliari, in Serie A. As a consequence, every match played in the provincial capital was like a highly charged anti-mainland independence celebration. If Cagliari had managed to win the league, Sardinians would have immediately seceded from the Second Republic of Italy and declared themselves a separate geopolitical entity. Or perhaps they would have invited Italy to join the newly formed Republic of Sardinia!

The story began when two local players, a full-back and a forward, from an amateur Sardinian club, Gonnostramazza, Andrea Casti, twenty-nine, and Fabio Curreli, twenty-five (the Italian media have a real 'thing' about people's ages, particularly *calciatori*, for whom age and marketability customarily go together) were traded to a rival local Sardinian club, l'Ales. But they weren't exchanged for cash. The two players were swapped for five new soccer balls. Amazingly, the reaction from locals was whether or not Gonnostramazza got a good deal! The local newspaper said the balls received in exchange for the two players were of a high-quality brand and cost 80 000 lire each. That's around US$35 or a grand total of US$175.

Gonnostramazza's coach and treasurer were certainly not very happy. In what was reported as a three-hour showdown, they argued vehemently with the team's manager — who, for some strange reason, had been appointed by the town's mayor — that they were being ripped off. Nevertheless, the exchange went ahead.

The norm in Italy is that amateur players' transfers do not involve the vulgar transaction of money, either in large or small amounts. But in this case, Gonnostramazza's deal-savvy manager said he could not bear to see his prized *difensore* and *attaccante* go without at least getting something in return. 'It's true that I asked for five balls in exchange for Casti and Curreli,' he admitted, a tinge ruefully. 'I wasn't going to let them go without a symbolic payment.'

The quote I borrowed from the Berlitz guide to open this chapter talked about Sundays being 'less sacred for mass in the morning than for soccer in the afternoon'. But towards the end of August 1999, when Bologna and Torino kicked off the first Serie A match for the 1999–2000 season, one of the most sacred customs in Italian life came to an end. Italian Sundays would never be the same again. *Calcio*, the national pastime, would still be played on Sundays, but not *exclusively* on Sundays.

For decades, as journalist Laura Collura pointed out, Italian football fans had arranged their weekends so they could devote the first part of each Sunday afternoon to their cherished soccer club. 'Wives and girlfriends knew they had no choice but to accept the fate of either tagging along to the stadium or sitting quietly while the men screamed and thrashed about with their ears pressed against a radio,' she said. In recent years, in what has been a major anthropological shift, Italian women, mainly the younger, more liberated ones, have begun to enjoy the Sunday soccer ritual too, 'becoming ardent fans like their male companions and mates'.

So what has brought about this change in the habits of not so much a lifetime, but an entire nation's lifestyle? One word — television. Or, to be more precise, two words — television rights. The burgeoning, ferociously competitive and highly lucrative market for soccer broadcast rights was, in Collura's words, about to 'reorganise the Italian week'. From now on, Serie A and Serie B fixtures would be staggered over three days, from Friday night through to Monday night.

'Soccer enthusiasts,' wrote Collura, 'will be forced to check the schedule week by week in order to follow the progress of their team and of its rivals. For Italians, the new timetable means a veritable cultural revolution.'

On the face of it, an outsider ignorant of the mores underpinning the game might have thought the changes would be a bonus to Italy's hordes of almost certifiable soccer maniacs. In addition to the European and international club competitions and other tournaments that are usually played midweek, this would mean more soccer than ever. *Tifosi* heaven, one would have thought. But not for the Italians, besotted not just by the game, but, more particularly, by their clubs.

As an immediate consequence of the new arrangements, the danger, as social rather than sports commentators saw it, was that soccer could lose its national allure as a special event and become an everyday affair. According to Laura Collura, even before the opening kick-off under the new schedule, 'the novelty had prompted a flood of protests, angry editorials and cries of nostalgia for the good old times'.

Back in the 1960s, Italian pop star Rita Pavone had a huge hit with a song about a woman, a soccer widow if you like, who moaned about being left at home alone every Sunday when her footy fanatic husband went off to the stadium. After the announcement of the scheduling changes, Pavone, still around and performing, reminded her fans that she used to sing 'On Sunday you always leave me alone.' 'Now,' she said, 'I'll have to write a new song called "Sad Saturday"!' When football makes it into the pop music arena, you know you're dealing with a formidable sociological issue.

The *Italy Daily* reported that Federcasalinghe, a national housewives' organisation, had expressed dissatisfaction with what it dubbed 'the new-fangled schedule of their husbands' week'. Psychologists and behaviouralists leapt on the bandwagon of national discontent. Too much soccer on TV could 'cloy' viewers, some said. Overdose them, turn them off. Others saw the changes having a potentially damaging impact, would you believe, on Italians' sex lives. For women, said Maria Rita Parsi, a psychologist, 'too much soccer could prove more intrusive than a rival in love'. One early poll actually found three out of ten Italian women believed they would be far more likely 'to seek out amorous conquests' if their husbands or boyfriends insisted on being soccer junkies. More predictably, movie theatre managers groaned that so many more football matches on television would adversely affect their business.

'Greed, nothing but greed,' was a common reaction to the television-prompted changes. There was certainly big money at stake — 570 billion lire (US$252 million) over six years from the pay-TV networks to the popular Turin-based Juventus club, 480 billion respectively to AC Milan and Inter Milan, 400 billion respectively to Lazio and Roma, 360 billion to Fiorentina, 280 million to Parma, and even 180 million to Serie B team Napoli.

The soccer commentators and editorial writers chimed in. Giorgio Tosatti from the leftish *Corriere della Sera* reckoned the 'thirst for money' did not bode well for the sport. Tosatti figured that the changes indicated that despite apparent widespread riches, clubs were still having trouble making financial ends meet. 'They pour everything they earn into the pockets of players, coaches, mediators, managers and the composite fauna that lives in the soccer zoo,' he wrote. 'It's not by chance that their books are all in the red.'

Tosatti's most biting criticism of the new weekend spread of fixtures was that the new regime offered more matches, but only on paper. In reality, he argued, only Italians able to afford the expensive pay-TV subscriptions would be able watch it all: 'To watch every game a chosen team plays, fans might have to sign up for both Telepiu and Stream. Turning soccer into a show available only to those who can afford to buy pay-TV services could estrange part of the audience.'

Tosatti, in fact, had introduced a highly relevant political consideration into the argument, reflecting a growing fear that the historically egalitarian appeal of Italian soccer could be undermined by selective, pay-to-view support for teams. 'The success of soccer is also linked to its ritual aspects (with everyone still considering it a regular Sunday event), its simplicity, punctuality and immediacy. Now it's becoming incomprehensible,' he wrote. On the other hand, Laura Collura claimed that despite the widespread and heated protests, many Italians were unfazed. 'They are confident,' she wrote, 'that the soccer tradition is strong enough to withstand even these drastic changes.'

She was backed up by psychoanalyst Aldo Carotenuto, who added that while Italians were generally concerned about the changes and the avarice of the football-hungry media moguls, there was no risk of a soccer overdose. Quite the opposite. 'If television could air soccer twenty-four hours a day,' he said, 'everyone would be happier. The more games television will offer, the more the audience will ask for.'

From the Proletariat to Presidents

In early June 1999, I found myself on assignment at the European Commission headquarters in Brussels. In my ongoing capacity as an Australian television journalist, I'd been granted a rare one-on-one interview with the EC President-elect, Dr Romano Prodi. Up until late 1998, Prodi had enjoyed an unusually long run as Prime Minister of Italy.

My appointment with the intriguing if enigmatic Prodi was for eight in the evening at a predetermined location. The Australian TV crew — cameraman, sound recordist, producer and me — arrived well in advance, at least half an hour early, at the sparsely furnished, windowless interview room in the steel and glass EC block, one of the EU's many administrative adjuncts scattered through Brussels, the so-called 'EU city'.

To our enormous surprise and mild embarrassment, Prodi and his media advisor were already waiting. Prodi's response — after I'd made the usual stumbling apologies that one makes in these tricky situations where dignitaries are involved, even when no fault or blame can be apportioned — was effusive and friendly, almost cavalier. In fact, it was very Italian — which is what Prodi is, very Italian. Indeed, he greeted us like long-lost *amici*! The man about to be installed in one of the world's most powerful positions was not even vaguely put out. As he said, we were not late; he was early.

The crew began setting up. Indulging in some light banter, as you do in these circumstances, I told Prodi that it would take fifteen to twenty minutes to get the cameras and lights ready. Given the delay, I asked, in the politest possible way, if he might like to take a coffee break. We would let his assistant know when we were ready to start filming. Relaxed and jovial, the man staring Europe's arguably most thankless task in the face laughed heartily, adding with his wonderfully *profondo* Italian accent: 'Thank you. No one ever suggests that I should take a break! Quite the opposite! They think I should be doing something every minute of the day. Okay, I will take a break. I know it's very un-Italian of me, but I don't need a coffee. We Italians probably drink too much of it anyway. Let's have a bit of a chat — before we get too serious!'

And chat we did. He was extremely easy to converse with. Indeed, I quickly became frustrated that our cameras were not rolling then and there to capture the infectious informality of the man. The good 'academic' doctor's minder had obviously told him that I was taking a working sabbatical in Prodi's home country. He wanted to know why and where. When he got his answers, his tongue firmly in his cheek, he replied, 'Well, if you are living in San Giovanni Valdarno in Tuscany and I live in Bologna, why are we doing this interview in Brussels? We should do two interviews — one in Bologna, where the food is better, and another in San Giovanni Valdarno, where the wine is better.'

'Great idea!' I responded, warming to his natural, easygoing manner and conversational playfulness.

By now, Prodi was well into the small talk — or was it so small after all?

'Which team do you support — Fiorentina, I suppose?' he said, with a mock sneer. 'Bologna, Bologna!' he added quickly, jabbing himself in the chest to signal his allegiance. 'Have you been to wonderful Bologna?' Yes, we had. 'Did you like it?' Very much. 'Why?' I began to wonder who was supposed to be asking the questions. Why? Any number of reasons. The politics for one. It is known as the 'Red Centre' after all, an irresistible lure for a political journalist. 'Sure. What else?' Well, definitely its famous food and, of course, the football! 'Ahhh! The football.' Another cheeky smile broke out on his face. 'Bologna *tre*, Fiorentina *zero*,' he grinned, giving me the result of the most recent match between the two teams.

'I know. My sons and I were there. It was a disaster,' I grimaced.

The Boys on the Bologna Bus

The last time I was with the 'boys on the bus' was in California during Ronald Reagan's Presidential campaign back in the early 1980s. It was great fun being an inexperienced member of such a ruthlessly ambitious group as the White House press corps. If they had had chainsaws, they would have cut each other to shreds to get to the story-of-the-day first. Nice guys all, but ferociously competitive — a bit like our travelling companions on the bus to Bologna that wet Sunday afternoon. They were on it for one reason and one reason alone — the match between Fiorentina and Bologna.

During the three-hour trip, Pierluigi, his girlfriend Monica, and their friend, Ricardo, took it upon themselves to calm the obvious nerves and anxiety etched on the faces of the *australiano* and his two young sons. Despite their fractured English and our even more fractured Italian, they proved valuable information sources and guides. They've remained friends, by the way.

Our two boys have since been to matches with one or all three of them (without their parents present) and returned to our adopted nest in San Giovanni Valdarno without a scratch or a bad memory!

But that trip to Bologna would turn out to be one of those contemporary Italian experiences that only contemporary Italian soccer could contrive: the *carabiniere* check at the *autostrada* exit on the outskirts of the city, the *polizia* escort to the *stadio*, the cordoned-off streets, our designated 'away fans only' *entrata*, security guards taking the tops from our *acqua minerale* bottles, 'de-missiling' them in case any of us were silly enough to consider pitching them at the Bologna fans, and, of course, the armed riot squad lining the climb up into our designated (and segregated) area in the stand. A ten-metre high fenced enclosure separated us, the hundreds of

Piazza Masaccio, San Giovanni Valdarno. Why is the piazza so Italian — like ours in the *centro storico*? What is it about Italians that makes them want one in the first place? Are they maybe more 'centred' than the rest of us? And if they are, doesn't that tell you a lot — about both them and us?

Every day, old Italian men gather in 'their corner' of the piazza, outside the commune. They spend a lot of time talking about football, food and politics. They also spend a lot of time linking the present to the past. All Italians do; they reckon it will help them cope with the future.

One of life's more pleasantly bizarre ways to spend a Saturday afternoon — travelling by *vaporetto* (water bus) to a football match in Venice. *Calcio* and *canali* — two cultures meeting, but not clashing.

When you get to the football in Venice — or anywhere else where the national *Serie A campionato* is played — the riot police are already there. Despite international perceptions to the contrary, there's seldom any rioting for them to police.

In Italy and the world generally, there's plenty of near-hysterical carry-on about flares, punch-ups, injury and even death at football matches. But when you take into account the vast number of fans involved — probably billions, globally — football violence pales into insignificance in the 'man's inhumanity to man' stakes.

What's behind the masks of Venice? More to the point, what's behind the attractiveness of the legendary Italian way? Maybe it's because Italians are never surprised when democracy and party politics let them down; they're more surprised when they don't!

Forza Fiorentina! You don't have to be Italian to get excited about a match-winning 'Batigol' against arch-rivals, SS Lazio. It's one of those marvellously inexplicable passions.

Volterra, Toscana. What a location for a family romp.

Ned's *ottante-sette San Giovannese squadra*. When he warmed up to come off the bench in his first match, Kirsty told me I had a tear in my eye. She was right. In his blue rain-jacket, he was fulfilling his *papà*'s dream to be Italian — even for a while.

With *calcio*, it's always agony and ecstasy — even in an Umbrian backyard.

This is the real Tuscan Italy. Not a tourist in sight! And it was all of ten minutes drive from our *piccolo appartamento*. It's the Italy the faddish new globalised world and its IT-driven socio-economy shouldn't touch — unless it's to ensure the survival of enduring and desirable lifestyles, not consume them.

Every Saturday *mercato*, Lucia, Pippo and their girls came to town with the fruit and vegies we needed for the next few days. They also brought recipe suggestions and the latest political gossip.

This, would you believe, is the same Piazza Masaccio on the front cover of this book. The cover shot was taken much earlier in the day. When the Italians come together for *passeggiata* in the evenings, they *come together*. Non-Italians do a lot of talking about community; but Italians are One.

Why Italy? Try the simple, fresh, seasonal food and cheap, drinkable wine — and, of course, the always exciting football and perpetually intriguing politics.

visiting Fiorentina fans, from the tens of thousands of Bologna fans. The heavy steel and thick reinforced glass barricade was necessary, according to the game's authorities, to prevent violent exchanges between rival fans. Everyone's heard about soccer violence, but very few have actually been touched by it. Even fewer participate. However, the threat is always there. Unfortunate incidents do happen. Precautions must be taken.

That day and on other match days, the only trouble we experienced — apart from the odd 500 lire coin or half-full plastic bottle hurled into our enclosure — was silly verbal abuse from opposition supporters on the other side of the wire and glass. In recent years, of course, there have been seriously violent clashes, awful injuries and even deaths. However, at least for this particular match, the melodramatic antagonism on either side of the fence was more theatre than a trigger for potential violence. Most of the time, that's all it is. At football matches, going to or from them, or elsewhere, Italians can be almost overwhelming in their hospitality and geniality. But when violence — stabbings, shootings, punch-ups, vandalism and the like — actually does break out, before, during or after matches, individuals do suffer, football is blamed and all of Italy must reflect on this most undesirable and negative aspect of its single greatest national passion.

But even in Bologna on that wet, grey April afternoon, the inherent link between football and politics was clearly demonstrated once again. The packed Stadio Renato

Dall'Ara was only a few hundred kilometres but a world away from the agonies then taking place in Kosovo. But when the two teams and the match officials took to the field prior to the kick-off, for those few tense moments when all eyes in the crowd and at home were on the centre of the pitch, they were all wearing — over their playing strips and official's garb — specially prepared T-shirts advocating 'Pace a Kosovo'. *Pace*, as you probably didn't need to be told, is Italian for peace. In most countries, this sort of statement would be regarded as far too loaded and political, particularly at a football match. But not in Italy.

The Dark Side of the Football Moon

There are many people who believe the recent transformation of European soccer into a bigger and bigger business has cast a dark shadow on the game's progress as a social, as distinct from commercial, agent. Has it, they ask, served to heighten the frustrations, insecurities and racial prejudices of Italy and the rest of the continent's less enlightened and deprived? Has the commercialisation and corporatisation of the world's most popular and powerful sport indirectly provoked hooliganism and violence among a tiny minority of hardline fanatics? Has it provided reasons for the so-called socio-economic 'underclass' to besmirch the game's otherwise clean image and reputation?

In the United Kingdom, studies certainly contend that this could well be the case. The crack anti-hooligan and anti-Nazi squads at Scotland Yard, who work together because they often find themselves dealing with the same culprits, along with their German and Dutch police counterparts, are in the frontline of the fight against hooliganism on a weekly basis. In Italy, it is estimated that hardline hooligans number less than 5000. Some even put the figure as low as 3500. Compared to the 30 million or so self-professed *calcio* supporters throughout the country, they are very few. But their public impact far surpasses their small representation. It is precisely this problem that has given rise to the perception that Italy is a hotbed of soccer hooliganism.

Those very Australian sporting quipsters HG Nelson and Rampaging Roy Slaven have often joked that the explanation for soccer violence and hooliganism is because 'the game itself on the field is so bloody boring!' If only it were that simple. In reality, soccer violence — or at least the propensity for it from a tiny minority — is not a sporting phenomenon. It's a socio-economic, dare I say, even political one.

Ironically, it is Lazio, the same aggressively entrepreneurial Serie A club that launched itself onto the Italian stockmarket and into the world of big business, that provides the most stark evidence of the game's darker side.

The 1998–99 season finished on a very sombre note when, in May 1999, four Salernitana supporters were burned to death on a special fans-only train taking them home after defeat in a Serie A match. The fire had been deliberately lit by other Salernitana fans, angry at the result, a loss that made it impossible for the struggling southern club to avoid humiliating relegation to Serie B. The Italian Government reacted by introducing strict controls and even bans on travel by away-club supporters. But many asked if the Salernitana tragedy was an ominous sign of things to come.

At the start of the 1999–2000 season, when the star-studded Lazio first XI played newly promoted but ultimately relegated Torino, the visitors from the northern city dominated by the giant Fiat Corporation included a black player from Senegal in their side, Dijbril Diawara. The Lazio supporters subjected the African to a deluge of racist taunts. As the *Italy Daily* reported: 'True to their hard-right reputation, SS Lazio skinheads waved banners showing Nazi insignia and Celtic crosses while they jeered obscene insults at ... Diawara.'

According to the same report, apart from the four Salernitana train deaths, at least 900 Italian soccer fans were injured in violent clashes the previous season. This usually happened during 'running battles' following lower level Serie B and Serie C matches — the lower the level, the greater the potential for violence, perhaps?

But on Serie A 'ultras', the tag given to the most fanatical fans, like the *Irriducibili* from Lazio, *Italy Daily's* Nicholas Rigillo and Kathryn Hone had an interesting perspective, putting the whole issue of soccer violence in a political and financial context. 'The ultras' enemies are not only the fans of rival teams,' they commented, 'but can even be their own clubs. This is due in part to a widening gap between professional clubs, mesmerised by the financial windfall that has enriched the sport in recent years, and their hardline fans, many of them from poor, frustrated backgrounds.' Rigillo and Hone recalled that in the 1970s — Italy's so-called 'Years of Lead' when terrorism dogged the country — the atmosphere inside the stadiums was extremely tense as Italy's football fans organised themselves along political lines. Apparently, some of the old labels still survive, witnessed by the existence of AC Milan's Brigate Rossonere, based on the old left-wing terrorist group the Red Brigades, and Inter Milan's Boys SAN, which stands for *Squadre Armate Neroazzure* or Armed Black and Blue Squads.

Stadiums are definitely much safer these days than in the late 1970s and early 1980s, when throwing seats and urinating from the stands on other fans was commonplace. 'It was quite frightening,' remembered one longtime Inter fan. 'But you can't get rid of that behaviour completely. Fans are a mirror of the society outside, and outside there are racists, violent people and idiots.' But as Rigillo and Hone recognised, the influence of the fans may be on the wane in a sport increasingly dominated by money: 'The *Irriducibili* — 5000 hardcore supporters who dedicate their lives to soccer — feel that they are being pushed to the margins by the sport's transformation into big business.' The argument is that Lazio president Sergio Cragnotti wants to turn attendance at the club's homeground, the Stadio Olimpico on the outskirts of Rome, into 'an elitist affair'.

As a result, say Rigillo and Hone, Lazio's hardened *Irriducibili* 'are dangerously close to the edge'. They figure that the stark contrast between Cragnotti's ambitious business plans and those of the *Irriducibili* are made even more obvious by a visit to the fans' headquarters, a dark and humid basement adorned with anti-government graffiti. 'Those who frequent it,' write Rigillo and Hone, 'consider it their real home, a retreat from the shabby Roman neighbourhoods in which they have been brought up. Though officially apolitical, the *Irriducibili* are mostly right-wing, poor and angry.'

'Yes, there are some people who are frustrated and display Nazi banners and we're not going to do anything to stop it,' says Stefano Marinelli, one of the club's leaders. 'Of course, we sympathise with the Right. What has that got to do with anything?' In the long run, everything, I would have thought. In the old days, we called it working-class false consciousness.

What was that innocent comment made by Colin Firth's fanatical Arsenal fan's well-meaning girlfriend in that marvellous British film *Fever Pitch*? She was trying to console him after his mighty Gunners had lost a vital FA Cup match. It was an impossible task she had set herself and her one real attempt sent him right off. 'Don't get so upset, honey,' she said. 'It's just a game.' Oh, yeah!

By early 2000, the *Irriducibili*'s extreme behaviour at matches had become a full-blown political issue, with media coverage to match. It quickly became a problem not just for the Lazio club, but for the centre-left Italian government and, needless to say, for soccer in general.

The trouble boiled over when at a televised Serie A match at the Stadio Olimpico, the *Irriducibili* unfurled a huge banner glorifying the late Serbian war criminal Arkan, a paramilitary leader who had been shot dead in Belgrade a few weeks before. 'The provocation fuelled worries that hateful and racist displays, which have increasingly become a fixture in the stadium, risked turning Italy's favourite sport into a forum for reactionary propaganda,' wrote Christopher Emsden in the *Italy Daily*. It's worth pointing out that in the Lazio squad that day were two Croats and a Serb.

The incident and its political ramifications were discussed and argued in the national parliament. The then Prime Minister Massimo D'Alema got heavily involved in the debate and the Mayor of Rome, Francesco Rutelli, called for immediate intervention. Sergio Cragnotti declared that some of Lazio's fans had evidently decided to exceed 'every threshold of good taste'. He promised that Lazio and he personally would 'actively collaborate with all means at our disposal to extirpate racial intolerance and politicisation from the club's stadium. Cragnotti was, in effect, demanding that politics be kept out of sport. Fat chance in Italy. What he was dealing with was its inevitable mix at its very worst.

Darwin Pastorin, the author of *Le Partite Non Finiscono Mai* or *The Games Never Finish*, went so far as to warn that Lazio's 'virulent fans' could sound the death knell of Italy's otherwise colourful and peaceful stadium culture. 'Fan banners have a long history and were certainly always meant to be rude,' he said. 'But they used to be more ironic and reflected the usual medieval allegiance to one's hometown.' According to Pastorin, the days when Napoli fans waved signs in front of visiting Verona supporters, claiming to have stolen away with Romeo's sweetheart Juliet, were well and truly gone. Today, some of Italy's stadiums have become 'dens of hatred', or as Emsden sees it, they are becoming inhabited by angry and frustrated people inclined to spend their Sunday afternoons 'exalting such icons of violence as Arkan'.

The last word from Darwin Pastorin has a relevance that goes beyond football, beyond what the Italian authorities might do to curb this political plague, even beyond Arkan's self-appointed killer thugs known as the 'Tigers', and maybe even beyond the mayhem of the Balkans.

'You can't give an intelligent interpretation to something stupid,' he said.

Italy's Soccer Fans are Strikers Too!

The author's first 'real job' in journalism, just on thirty years ago, was as the industrial roundsman for the national newspaper the *Australian*, Murdoch-owned long before his entry into international television, let alone the ludicrously lucrative soccer broadcast market. For twelve months or so, daily life for yours truly was almost non-stop reportage and involvement in industrial politics and affairs, union disputes, lock-outs, sit-ins and strikes, from piddling ones over piddling workplace matters to serious national stoppages that would bring the country grinding to a halt and pitted Australian against Australian. I also reported some very *strange* workers' disputes and strikes. But none as odd as the strike by Fiorentina fans halfway through the 1999–2000 season.

Tens of thousands of them were physically present in Florence's Stadio Artemio Franchi for Fiorentina's match against the southerners from Calabria, Reggina, yet they were all silent, deliberately silent. None of their usual well-rehearsed chanting, singing, whistling. No orchestrated noisy encouragement of the players. No flares. No explosive bangers. No abusive jeering at the Reggina supporters over in their special enclosure. All they were was *there*. It was eerie, compared to the pre-match pandemonium we usually found ourselves caught up in at Fiorentina's home games. It was a protest, but a protest about what and against whom?

Fiorentina's fans had a grievance and they wanted the bosses of the club to know about it. It was about football, so it had to be at a football match, yet it was also a stunning illustration of the undeniable connection between Italian football and Italian politics, in this case, industrial politics.

Halfway through the 1999–2000 Serie A season, Fiorentina was, according to its normally devoted one-eyed fans, playing like shit, *giocava di merda* — a particularly derogatory Italian term usually reserved for the opposing club and its players, not your own side! But Fiorentina had slipped badly into the bottom half of the championship ladder. For team, owner, club and fans alike, the real fear was that relegation into the second division, Serie B, was not out of the question. Horror of horrors! Shame of shames! An impossible thought! A horrible nightmare! Life out of Serie A would not be life! For an irrationally committed Italian soccer fan, it was that serious.

So according to Fiorentina's thousands of normally loyal followers, our new friends, something had to be done and done quickly. Relegation loomed on the football horizon. It was a drastic problem that demanded a drastic solution. But interestingly, their protest, their *dimostrazione pubblica*, was not directed against the club's players. The blame was being directed elsewhere.

As the fans saw it, Fiorentina's owner and sole financial benefactor, Vittorio Cecchi Gori, was the root cause of the problem. The squad's coach, Giovanni Trapattoni, who would eventually resign and is now coach of Italy, was also copping flak. What was the problem, the source of the fans' grievances? In a few words, player purchases, inconsistent performances and curious team selections. According to the fans — who have no difficulty articulating the problems as they see them — some of Trapattoni's player selections and positional changes had the players themselves, the soccer media and the team's supporters bemused. Their fundamental complaint was that 'Trap', for all his experience and success over the years, had lost the plot, at training and in the coach's dugout. He was at a total loss to come up with an explanation for the inconsistency of Batistuta and his boys.

A few weeks earlier, they had beaten two of the game's giants, mighty treble-winners Manchester United and Arsenal, in the European Champions League. The team from the 'City of David' also performed well against local Goliaths like Juventus, AC Milan and Inter but they failed to get their act together to knock over lowly Italian minnows such as Venezia, Bari and Lecce. As for Cecchi Gori, Florentines from every walk of that city's interesting life were demanding he pull out his considerable chequebook and buy specialist players for key positions.

This particular afternoon, the fans' placards and banners were not the usual stirring stuff: 'Vittorio, Words! Words! Words! ... I've Got Lots of Players In My Pocket You Keep Telling Us — Yes! But They Are All Panini Figurines!'

(Panini figurines are soccer cards with players' pictures on them that kids collect and swap.) And this one: 'We're Present Only For Florence!'

The fans' protests had actually started at the previous match and spread over to the midweek match against Venezia in the Coppa Italia, the Italian Cup, which they threatened to boycott. Faced with the real possibility of a near-empty stadium, Cecchi Gori responded by opening up the gates for 1000 lire a ticket, about US50 cents, one thirtieth the normal midweek Coppa Italia ticket price. Some fans took up the cheap offer but did not barrack or cheer on the team in its disappointing 1–1 draw. Others were livid. They couldn't be bribed by what they saw as a football version of 'thirty pieces of silver'.

These were the fans who, before the Reggina match, organised all the diehard supporters in the popular standing room-only Curva Fiesole and Curva Marione behind the goals to unfurl super-large printouts of a 1000 lire note as the Fiorentina players walked onto the field. Everyone did, including yours truly and his thirteen-year-old *tifoso* son. The placard that went with it had all the political hallmarks of a union rally: 'A Thousand Lire To Buy the Silence of Those Who Want to Protest!'

This old industrial reporter took the point, but thought it might have been a bit more complex than that. My son Ned disagreed. 'I'm glad we're not protesting against the team,' he said. 'It's not the players' fault. They're doing the best they can under the circumstances. Trap, I'm not sure about. But Cecchi Gori can't have it both ways. He can't own the team and not buy players when they need to. I'm with the fans.'

'I can't imagine this happening at home in Australia, can you?' I said. Ned agreed.

Early in the second half, Batistuta scored Fiorentina's sole and winning goal. The fans would normally have reacted with hysterical fervour: 'Batigol! Batigol! Batigol!' On this afternoon, they merely clapped, politely. However, they were suppressing their secret relief. So were young Ned and I. What were we watching — the politics of football, the politics of being a fan, or perhaps just the politics of being an Italian?

PART THREE

FOOD FOR THE MIND

'In Italy, we don't eat to live, we live to eat!'

An Anonymous Italian Friend

'Globalisation does not mean that everyone eats the same hamburgers. It means that everyone has different views on the same things.'

Giuliano Amato, Italian Prime Minister

Who Said There Was No Such Thing as a Free Lunch?

Perched on a ridge deep in the Colline di Chianti, the much-celebrated wooded hills between Florence and Siena, there's a rambling hill town called Panzano. In spring and summer, like every other Tuscan town or village and its surrounding countryside, Panzano is invaded by *turisti stranieri*, foreign tourists, always well-intentioned but inescapably intrusive. Panzano is the sort of place travellers to Italy find irresistible, and why not? It is classically seductive, the very reason they venture to Tuscany in the first place.

But in winter, Panzano-in-Chianti, like the rest of Tuscany, while never completely free of jet-setting, jet-lagged and backpacking outsiders, receives travellers of the less-intrusive local kind. Every Sunday, Panzano, or more specifically one particular shop in the town, plays host to a delightfully deviant kind of attraction. Tucked away in an unassuming back lane is, at first sight, an uncomplicated *macelleria*, a butcher's shop. In itself, this is not exactly an exceptional discovery in any Italian town or village. Most Italian butcher's shops are pretty special in their own often unrefrigerated fashion. But this one is *molto speciale*. Its suitably weathered shingle announces it as 'Antica Macelleria Cecchini' which, very roughly translated, means the 'antique butcher shop of Cecchini'.

Dario Cecchini is both its proprietor and its main meat man. He refers to his establishment not as a run-of-the-mill *macelleria*, but as an artisan's *bottega*, a workshop. His business partner, Laura Torio, as American expat as Panzano is classically Chianti, says that Dario runs his establishment 'with the same passion as an artist runs his studio'. 'Dario and his shop both maintain the tradition of hospitality offered for generations,' she enthuses. Hospitality? We're talking about a highly marketable business here, a shop that sells meat, lots of meat, expensive Tuscan meat, hand-fed or hunted.

So what has selling great chunks of raw beef and pork got to do with hospitality, even legendary Tuscan hospitality? Every Sunday — the best day to visit Panzano and Dario's *bottega* in particular — the lane outside Antica Macelleria Cecchini swarms with smartly casual Italians. Somehow or other in Panzano's labyrinthine lanes, they've managed to find a park for their Fiat Puntos or sleek Ferraris for a couple of hours. Sunday morning in Panzano is really an Italian version of a 'butcher's picnic', with one striking difference. Every weekend, Dario, his staff and partners turn on delectable meat-based food — for free! His shop is jammed with customers from as far away as Florence and even Rome, a good three- to four-hour drive via the A1 *autostrada*. More often than not six-deep, these *carne*-cranks are buying up big for the working week ahead back in the city. But as well as the *macelleria* itself, there's an adjoining store a bit like an open-plan delicatessen. Here, another usually even larger gathering of affably rambunctious and dedicated carnivores shoulder their way to the counter to obtain plates of that particular Sunday's delights. In scattered wicker baskets, rough-hewn crusty Tuscan bread is there for the taking and lashings of cheap but eminently drinkable *vino rosso locale* is available to all in customary straw-bound two-litre casks. The food-proud Tuscans won't like to hear this, but they actually make pretty ordinary bread, usually saltless and, dare I suggest it, tasteless.

As it turned out, our wintry Sunday was a taste experience as distinct from a taste sensation. Ours was a *giorno di trippa e altri intestini*, a tripe and other intestines day. For the courageous, the foolhardy, the adventurous and the manifestly curious gathered in Panzano on that brisk *domenica mattina*, there was a tripe gallantine, piquant tripe, unadulterated boiled tripe and *panini di trippa*, tripe sandwiches. However, in the ultimate non-gourmand analysis, it was still the lining of a dead cow's stomach. Remember your own hesitant first encounter with tripe, and you will know what I mean.

Food and Politics — Not on an Empty Stomach

Laura Torio, a modern meat marketer if ever there was one, provides a set of gastronomic guidelines for the packs of hungry foodies who make the Mecca-like pilgrimage to out-of-the-way Panzano every Sunday morning. 'Greet Dario with a *buongiorno* or *buonasera*. It is considered polite to greet everyone as you walk in,' exhorts her cautiously patronising notes. 'Relax and enjoy. This is not the place to be in a hurry.'

A typical shopping spree at the Antica Macelleria Cecchini can take up to an hour. Laura tells potential clients that when it's their turn, they'll be able to take as much time as they like. But with the artists at work in the kitchen and at the chopping block, she urges that customers ask before taking photographs, *'Posso'* or 'May I?' being the accepted form of politeness. 'After too many flashes, it's not fun anymore,' she points out.

The array of meat and meat-based dishes prepared on site is mouth-wateringly typical Tuscan fare and the available selections vary with the seasons and Dario's culinary predilections: pâtés of wild boar, of course — *the* Tuscan speciality — lamb, guinea hen with hazelnuts, terrines featuring chard pork and prunes ('Incredible!' coos Laura), *spiedini*, skewers of the famous super-tender, super-expensive

Chianina beef — best eaten raw or very lightly grilled, Dario's answer to sushi and *salsicce*, ubiquitous in Italy but varying in their basic meat ingredient from region to region; in Panzano's case it's basically garlic sausages, beef and pork, but sometimes even turkey and ginger or lamb.

If you go to Florence, Tuscany or Dario's back lane meat-eaters' paradise in Panzano without literally sinking your teeth into a delectable slab of *bistecca alla fiorentina* or the *tagliata*, then not only haven't you really eaten, you haven't really lived! The bovine equivalent of milk-fed baby lamb, Chianina beef is one of the best beefs available anywhere in the world. Red meat devotees will tell you that it's up there with Japan's famous and much-prized Kobe beef. Price-wise, it's also in the same league.

'You'll notice that it's not marbled with fat,' Laura tells me. 'This means it must be cooked rare to be enjoyed at its best.' Did she say 'rare'? To take on a cut of Chianina beef, you need to be either ravenous or a pathological carnivore. The cuts are simply colossal, about two pounds — almost a kilo. And that's for one eater. It's best cooked on a barbecue. Barbecues, by the way, are one of Tuscany's, if not Italy's, best-kept culinary secrets. Always charcoal-fired, they definitely rival their 'barbie' counterparts in places like Texas and even Tenterfield. But I have to say, I've never seen or even heard of either amateur or professional barbecue chefs letting their favoured T-bone steaks 'breathe' for at least an hour at room temperature before cooking them. At the Cecchini *carne* establishment in Chianti, they insist that this is the only way to do it. Then they cook it for only four to five minutes on each side. Remember that these great two-pound chunks of *bistecca* can be a couple of inches thick. No wonder they are eaten rare, or more to the point, blue, the culinary term for bloody-near-still-kicking. In contrast, not just in colour, but tastiness, the US and Australian varieties are usually overcooked to the point of tasting like shoe leather.

In case you're a trifle squeamish about eating a half-alive, near-raw cow, Dario and Laura recommend letting your cut rest for fifteen minutes or so in a warm oven at around 140°C. Serve it simply with salt and top-quality extra-virgin oil. 'But please taste it first,' pleads Laura. 'The flavour is really amazing.' She's right. My wallet's audible groaning made it quite clear it was unconvinced of the true value of it all, yet should you ever make it to Panzano you should try it at least once.

What else can I tempt you with from Panzano? How about *tonno di chianti* — 'a play on words', as Laura puts it, before explaining that what appears to be tuna is, in fact, pork, slow-cooked in wine and herbs and then packed in oil, the way Italians preserve tuna. When they serve the pork, drizzled in the mandatory extra-virgin oil, they often eat it with a boiled bean salad. They also offer something they refer to as *profumo di chianti*, a mixture of salt and various herbs 'with the flavour and fragrance of the Chianti Hills', which is sprinkled on anything on a plate, or in a pan or a pot. 'Use it everywhere,' they advise.

The tantalising list of Panzano's delights goes on and on. *Mostarda mediterranea*, for instance, consists of a marvellous concoction of spicy bell-peppers served with a special pecorino sheep's cheese made in the traditional method, but using the 'choke', the head, of wild artichokes to coagulate the cheese and give it a nutty flavour.

The ultimate point of this deliberate taste treat is to prove the veracity of the anonymous quote that opens this chapter. If you're not convinced after visiting Panzano-in-Chianti, you must be hooked on fast food.

The Slow Food Movement — More Than Clever Wordplay?

'Food, as we all know, is the world's greatest cure for hunger.' Don't have a clue where this little bauble was picked up, but for years I've been carrying it around in my journalistic verbal kit-bag. It's not a bad line as throwaways go. But you would never convince an Italian that a cure for hunger is all that food is, or even close to it. For reasons that go way beyond the mere satiation of hunger, the Italians' celebration of food and their loving consumption of it are self-evident to any visitor. But how does it touch on their other great national passion of politics?

Back in 1986, a guy called Carlo Petrini and a bunch of his gastronomically oriented friends started something which, at least at first, was a bit of a joke. Today, fifteen years and a lot of meals later, it is the engine room of an international chorus of dissent against global technology, genetic engineering, economics, politics and corporatism — basically all the bugbears of the anti-globalisation crusade.

The deliciously named 'Slow Food' movement had its beginnings on the steps of Rome's beloved Piazza di Spagna, the Spanish Steps. Anyone who has been to Rome and hasn't walked, at least once, both up and down the Spanish Steps — with or without its pink azaleas in spring, its lovers, peddlers, guitar-playing backpackers and fabulous fashion models — hasn't really been to Rome! Despite its overwhelming allure for tourists and travellers the world over, it's one of those 'must sees' of not just Italy, but anywhere. For most of the postwar years, an American Express *cambio* on the edge of the piazza has been a conspicuous symbol of Italy's annual invasion by teenage hordes from elsewhere, particularly Americans, usually senior high school graduates.

At least that was the case until word got out that the 'two arches' were on their way to Bella Italia. 'Big Mac' was in town and hungry for space. He found it within a spray of the piazza's seventeenth-century marble Fontana della Barcaccia, designed by Bernini's father, Pietro. The whole idea of a McDonald's in Rome, let alone bang in the centre of the Piazza di Spagna, was anathema to Carlo Petrini and his Italian foodie mates. Hence their unprecedented anti-Maccas protest.

'It was just a game at first,' says Petrini. 'It was a chance to remind people that food is a perishable art, as pleasurable in its way as a sculpture by Michelangelo or a painting by Titian. We proclaimed it was time to get back to the two-hour lunch and the four-hour dinner.' Even some of Slow Food's supporters might wonder about that, but their message was clear.

The 1986 protest against McDonald's in the heart of Rome was the spark for a Europe-wide movement that is growing bigger and bigger. Indeed, the Arcigola Slow Food Movement, formally founded at a gathering in Paris in December 1989, is now seen as an international rallying point for like-minded foodies and then some!

In fact, in Europe over the past twelve years, it has been transformed into a genuine political movement. Slow Food has also emerged as a force in unlikely Japan and is said to even be taking a hold in the United States, the home of the almost universally maligned fast variety of food. Late in 2000, Slow Food had more than 400 official branches or *convivie* in Italy and 60 000 paid-up members. Its leaders claim international representation, with tens of thousands of members in thirty-five countries including Australia.

The association has an emerging but clearly identifiable political ideology to go with its love of good food for its own sake. Its purpose, it says, is 'to work to create an atmosphere of conviviality, valuing time, the so-called slow life philosophy, and sharing an appreciation for great food and wine'. When it came into being at the Opéra Comique in Paris in 1989, the representatives of the various member countries got together under the less catchy, more political slogan of 'For the Defense of and the Right to Pleasure'. As Petrini sees it, Slow Food was an inevitable backlash against what he described as 'societal velocity and homogenised, industrial grub'.

These days, all over Italy and in many European cities and towns, members of the movement meet for marathon meals and talk food, wine, culture, philosophy and, in its Italian *convivie* you can be assured, politics and football. Sounds like a normal journalistic long lunch! But journalists don't have a political manifesto — except not to have one! Slow Food has one and promotes it aggressively. Its credo makes fascinating and highly relevant reading in the contemporary context of the 'mushrooming' worldwide debate about the pros and cons of the global economy, free trade, e-commerce and the turbo-market.

'We are enslaved by speed and we have all succumbed to the same insidious virus: Fast Life, which disrupts our habits, pervades the privacy of our homes and forces us to eat Fast Foods,' the manifesto reads. 'To be worthy of the name, Homo Sapiens should rid themselves of speed before it reduces them to a species in danger of extinction. A firm defence of quiet material pleasure is the only way to oppose the universal folly of the Fast Life. May suitable doses of guaranteed sensual pleasure and slow, long-lasting enjoyment preserve us from the contagion of the multitude who mistake frenzy for efficiency. Our defence should begin at the table with Slow Food. Let us rediscover the flavours and savours of regional cooking and banish the degrading effects of Fast Food. In the name of productivity, Fast Life has changed our way of living and threatens our environment and landscapes. So Slow Food is now the only truly progressive answer. That is what real culture is all about: developing taste rather than demeaning it. And what better way to set about this than an international exchange of experiences, knowledge, projects? Slow Food guarantees a better future.'

So the 'Slow Foodies' would have us believe that not eating fast food will help us discover the pleasures of 'slowness', help us to learn about and understand the divergent cultures of the world, and help us become more tolerant of others who eat and therefore live differently from ourselves. 'Slow living', if you go with their approach to things of the brain and of the belly, will lead to 'a happier, healthier and more fulfilling life'. Not only that, it might encourage better planned, environmentally friendly tourism, 'where the best places are to relax and recharge' and where consumers can be educated consumers about the marketplace by highlighting quality foods and wines.

Don't Stress Out — Take a Long Italian Lunch

As you can tell from its manifesto, whatever else it is, the Slow Food movement is definitely not a haven for wowsers or wowserism. It is unapologetically into gastronomy and conviviality. Some of its members no doubt liken their activities to *gastrosessualità*, gastrosexuality, the knowing combination of food, wine and all that follows thereafter — if you're lucky and haven't overeaten or downed too much *vino*! Slowness is certainly supposed to be pleasurable, but perhaps not Bacchanalian.

The heart of the movement are the aptly named *convivie*, small and large groups of individuals from all walks of life united in 'the Slow Food spirit'. Their role is to stir the pot, as it were, against Fast Food and all that it represents industrially, commercially, economically, socially, culturally and, ultimately, politically. Hence the original targeting of McDonald's in Rome, as the international epitome of all that it rails against. Across the border in France, its French counterpart has also made the famous 'two arches' its number one target.

Slow Food ranks esteemed playwright Dario Fo among its most active and outspoken members. It also enjoys the tacit approval of senior Italian politicians, including Massimo D'Alema, a friend of Carlo Petrini's and a self-styled foodie himself.

'We disdain the stressful fast life,' says Petrini, echoing the sentiments of a growing number of people throughout the world, including those thousands who kicked up such a fuss — and unfortunately 'overcooked' their protest by allowing a few anarcho-loons to kick down a few doors and smash windows — at the fateful World Trade Organisation meeting in Seattle, and more recently at the World Economic Forum in Melbourne and the summit of the International Monetary Fund and World Bank in Prague.

'Fast food is killing off the social aspects of food. It strips people of their food wealth and culture,' Petrini warns, rightly or wrongly. Think for a moment about that politically and economically loaded term 'food wealth'. In many ways yet to be properly debated, Slow Food is Italy's political response to the global diaspora of corporate America and its almost pathological need to thrust itself onto other nationalities and cultures in the name of freedom and progress.

Something Smells Across the Border in the Region of Roquefort

St-Pierre-De-Trivisy, a tiny village in the south-west of France with a population of just over 600, is the home of that remarkably pungent French *fromage*, Roquefort, which should only ever be consumed with a crusty baguette. Yet it has also become the hub for what has become and will continue to be an important international debate, a microcosm of the much wider and deeper socio-political and economic issues affecting the planet in the post-communist era.

Phillipe Folliot, St-Pierre-de-Trivisy's mayor, explained to the *Washington Post* in late August 1999 that Roquefort was made from the milk of only one breed of sheep, in only one place in France and in only one special way. 'Roquefort is the opposite of globalisation!' he proclaimed. 'Coca-Cola you can buy anywhere in the world and it is exactly the same.' Monsieur Folliot's fight for Roquefort cheese was, in his words, nothing less than a fight against 'the Americanisation of Europe'. In particular, he had decided to take on a US decision a month earlier to impose 100 per cent tariffs on a wide range of European food and luxury products, including his beloved and all too tempting Roquefort, which can only be labelled as such if it is ripened in the caves near the town of Roquefort, just outside St-Pierre-de-Trivisy.

The Americans claimed they were merely retaliating in kind to Europe's refusal to drop a ban on US beef raised with growth hormones. In the increasingly vociferous global outcry over so-called GMFs, or genetically modified foods, the Yanks were asking for trouble — and they got it!

The French response was swift, to the point and sure to get a headline. Folliot and his fellow councillors in St-Pierre-de-Trivisy whacked their own 100 per cent impost on Coke sold at the town's popular camping ground and recreation centre. Bang in the middle of the European summer, with the town buzzing with cheese-loving gourmet travellers, their cheeky act immediately doubled the price of Coke — a measure bound to have an impact on sales. Not only that, Folliot vowed that the village's largely symbolic Coke tax would remain in place until the US lifted its tax on Roquefort cheese.

St-Pierre took action against Coke because it couldn't think of a more effective way to express its displeasure. The French Government couldn't do the retaliating because the EU speaks for France and other European nations on trade and the EU had run out of avenues of protest. As for Roquefort's champion, M. Folliot, he said he singled out Coke because it was a 'symbol of the American multinational that wants to uniformise taste all over the planet'.

St-Pierre's ten producers of ewe's milk — the source of its famous stinking cheese — were crucial to the town's economy. 'But they were also standing up for France and things French,' wrote Ann Swardson in the *Washington Post*. 'They were standing up for food — natural food, pure food. And, by inference, the French way of life.' Indeed, as Folliot told Swardson, predictably over a classically rich French lunch of foie gras, pike, breast of duck, Roquefort, of course, sorbet and a vigorous *vin du pays*, 'In this corner of France, on our little mountain, eating is not just to live. It is conviviality, business. We have a saying around here. Decisions are always made between the cheese course and the dessert!'

Swardson pointed out that to those Europeans — and a growing number of others around the world, including the Japanese, protesting against the 'Land of the Free' and its decidedly unfree double-standard on free trade — that it didn't matter a hoot that the World Trade Organisation had ruled that EU countries could not block hormone-treated beef from the US and Canada. Nor did it appear to matter that after more than a decade of research, the EU has been unable to produce a skerrick of scientific evidence to prove that hormone-enhanced beef was harmful to human health. 'What is important, as M. Folliot and his fellow protestors see it, is that the Americans want to make the French eat food they do not want to eat,' she wrote. She also quoted one of St-Pierre's ten sheep farmers who, every day of the seven-month annual Roquefort production season, milks 300 ewes. 'My personal opinion is that this has been imposed upon us,' he told Swardson. 'Today it's ewe's milk, tomorrow it's meat, then someday it's fruit and vegetables.'

But the French backlash was not restricted to the ubiquitous Coke. In August 1999, Jose Bove, a Parisian-turned-sheep-farmer and leader of what the *International Herald Tribune* called 'a self-styled anti-imperialist revolt over food', gave himself up to police in the southern French town of Montpellier after he led a group of farmers in the wholesale ransacking of an unfinished McDonald's restaurant in nearby Millau. 'My struggle,' Bove told reporters, 'is a battle against globalisation and for the right of people to feed themselves as they choose.' Can the whole matter of what we put in our stomachs three times a day get more political than that?

During the Cold War the American preoccupation was to be and to be seen to be both the world's most preferred and dominant ideology and also its mightiest military power. If the near-total demise of communism in the last decade of the twentieth century is any measuring stick, the Americans have achieved their arguably well-meaning objectives. Now, with that self-proclaimed victory under its belt, the current American obsession is to be and to be seen to be the world's strongest economy, and the home of the world's most alluring economic philosophy.

The end result of this latest hang-up is that what has become widely known as 'globalisation' is now seen as dangerously close to the virtual 'Americanisation' of business, financial dealings, and even entire economies — all over the world. Call it the new colonialism. Call it the latest brand of US economic imperialism. The current food fracas witnessed in the likes of Italy, France and Japan, be it about GMF, McDonald's, Roquefort cheese or whatever, has not only become one of those new much sought-after political causes, a universal peg on which the Europeans can hang much more than complaint, it has become an ideological battleground in places like Italy and France, which is hardly surprising. The Italians and the French are, after all, the world's pre-eminent foodies. Europeans invariably discuss their politics over food and drink. So for their food and drink to become a political issue is not exactly unusual or unexpected.

The British journalist Martin Kettle, these days the Washington correspondent for *The Guardian*, tells a story about being in a trattoria in Rome and watching an American couple work themselves into a lather because the management couldn't bring them a bottle of ketchup. 'I have this nagging feeling that in a world of increasingly shared values, Europeans and Americans still don't get it about one another,' wrote Kettle. Don't agree with that completely. The Europeans probably have an idea of what the Americans, are about — they just don't like it. The Americans, meanwhile, can't understand why the Europeans won't stop being stubbornly European and become what they believe everyone secretly wants to be — *American*.

However, after living in Europe for a year, I concur with Kettle's view that 'from the way we think about food to the way we think about health and violence and perhaps even science, it is striking how often Americans and Europeans can find themselves not so much at odds as simply looking down different ends of the telescope'. But which one has the tunnel vision? That's possibly *the* question of the first decade of the new millennium. Who do the rest of us follow — the Americans racing frantically towards a global cyberheaven or the Europeans who are prepared to pick only the good bits out of 'e-nirvana'?

With their longer history and greater record of hastiness, errors and bad judgments, the Europeans are not automatically wedded to technological developments that have an air of 'the fad' about them. They're more instinctively suspicious of snake-oil salesmen. They don't necessarily see what's being flogged as guaranteed golden opportunities that will only come once, but rather as things that could turn out to be useful at some point in time.

As pig-headed or head-in-the-sand as it may appear, the Europeans aren't prepared to wilfully toss away their long-held rule of thumb, a rule that seems to apply to all Europe's nations, that no matter what machines, electronic or otherwise, can do for humankind, humankind itself is still what it's ultimately all about.

On this question of the mutual myopia that persists between the Europeans and Americans, Kettle quotes social scientist Seymour Martin Lipset, a man who has studied the legendary American tunnel vision. He calls it 'exceptionalism'. 'Those who only know one country know no country,' he commented, making a ton of sense. The lopsided American view of economic and political globalisation, as Kettle says, writes off the national differences as 'old-fashioned'. Most Americans couldn't give a hoot about the genetic modification of their food, yet as we have observed the Europeans are up in arms about it.

'From the earliest times, human societies were defined by their food rituals, and food remains to this day not merely the stuff of life but the very stuff of cultural identity and difference,' writes Kettle. 'Europeans still like to think of themselves as close to the soil, as farmers who just happen to have lived in cities for generations. Food connects Europeans with their history and their sense of themselves. American food — especially the meat that goes in the ubiquitous burger, reminds Europeans of what they have lost, even if the sense of loss is sometimes heavily sauced with hypocrisy.'

We are what we eat.

It All Started in Genoa

The Italian city of Genoa is a crowded, rambling place hanging off the northern coastal slopes of the bay of the same name. Although on the other side of the country and culturally worlds apart from Venice, Genoa is also a 'water town', made famous by the impact of the sea on its history, its people and its lifestyle.

'Hemmed in between the Apennine mountains and the sea, it has tended, like its historic rival Venice on the east coast, to turn its back on Italy to seek its fortune on the high seas,' is how travel writer Jack Altman saw this colourful, marginally grotty hill city. Today, wandering its seamy port district, with its maze of lanes and stairways, tired buildings, poky piazzas and aggressive street-sellers, is absorbing to some, slightly *pericoloso* to others.

The Lonely Planet guide to Italy came across a labyrinth of narrow alleys at the heart of the old city near the port that it described as 'a scrappy zone of some ill-repute, but undeniably interesting, full of visiting sailors, prostitutes, delinquents and longtime residents'. As the same guidebook noticed, you can turn a corner in old Genoa and stumble across a marvellous medieval *chiesa* or an opulent residence of a well-to-do Renaissance family, often turned into a museum or something else. In the area's *ristoranti* and bars, the smart set rubs shoulders with 'the seamier side of Genovese life', but at night, it is far less inviting. More Italian yin and yang.

The contrasts don't stop at the port. With the ornate architecture of its Renaissance past cheek-by-jowl with the likes of McDonald's and its garish attempts to attract still reluctant tourists, Genoa is one of those typically Italian melanges of old and new. It has had its heyday — its best years are definitely behind it. But unlike the folk of most half-dead cities, the Genovese are energetically trying to resuscitate the Ligurian capital, including its bustling port, Italy's largest and the crux of the city's identity.

It's true, though, that Genoa's past remains more obvious and relevant than either its present or its future. *La Superba*, 'the proud and haughty', they used to call it in its halcyon days as a mighty maritime republic. Not today. Most tourists, Italian or otherwise, usually bypass Genoa on the way to the more noticeably appealing coastal resorts to its south on the Italian Riviera and west to France and the painfully ostentatious Côte d'Azur.

But mention this much-maligned, oft-avoided place to anyone possessing even a passing acquaintance with Italy — or probably more significantly, the great discoveries and voyages of history — and their first word-association reaction would almost certainly be the same — Christopher Columbus, or Cristoforo Colombo as he is known to the Italians. Columbus has always been Genoa's favourite son and probably its most notable achiever. But, yet again, the inevitable Italian paradox undercuts every certainty, even this one.

Even though he died not knowing what he had found, Columbus, of course, was the discoverer of the so-called 'New World'. It was he who discovered the world is round, and who inspired that other great Italian mariner Amerigo Vespucci, who brought us the very name of 'America', to go East, after being assured that he wouldn't topple off the edge of an apparently flat planet Earth.

As a Genovese, Columbus did all of his great discovering under the patronage of Isabella, the far-sighted Queen of Spain. To their great historic loss, the Italians didn't want to know Columbus, let alone his loopy ideas about another 'world' across the Atlantic, a world he was certain oozed riches, human exotica and anthropological intrigue.

The end result of this Italian reluctance to patronise Columbus was that Spain, not Italy, eventually became a superpower on the proceeds of the riches discovered in the Americas. Nevertheless, with a degree of justification, the Genovese claim him as theirs. His interest in sailing and map-making did have its genesis in the port city. In the wake of Genoa's newfound self-promotional skills, you can actually visit the *casa di Colombo et sua famiglia* in Porta Soprana where he was said to have been born in 1451, and grew up and returned to die a sad, disgruntled figure who was never really given due credit for his remarkable, albeit obsessive exploits. His maritime knowledge and well-developed sea culture are said to have turned him into one of the greatest sailors of all times, 'daring to do what no one else dared to do', as the brochure you pick up at the door of the old Columbus family home proclaims.

These days there seems little doubt that Columbus was Genovese. The locals quote various Italian, Spanish and other historians to back up their claim to him, including the American Samuel Eliot Morison, whom they say confirmed once and for all that 'it all started in Genoa'. How far you go in defining just what 'it' was, of course, is entirely up to you and how far you are prepared to go back, historically, to explain the present from the past. But you could easily argue that back in 1492 had Cristoforo and his scurvy-ridden crews on the *Niña*, the *Pinta* and the *Santa María* not literally bumped into what eventually became the Bahamas,

Cuba and the islands of the West Indies, thinking they had, in fact, reached Asia and the East Indies, our world today might have been a very different place. Who knows, had Vespucci not followed Columbus, had the two Americas not been invaded and named after him, plenty of other monumental pluses and minuses of history in the 509 years since 1492 may not have eventuated.

Perish the thought, but there may not have been a McDonald's in Via San Lorenzo, Genoa's wonderfully colonnaded main drag. There may not have been a Best Western Metropole Hotel further down the same street. And there may not have been New York rap CDs on *offerta speciale* in the gigantic music store in the waterfront warehouse that also houses the Columbus Museum.

Columbus has almost singlehandedly sparked the port city's renewal over the past ten years or so. In 1992 the Genovese unblushingly exploited the 500th anniversary of his famous transatlantic voyage to stage its first international Expo in and around the port. But if you visit the port today, you'd have to say that the dock development has more of a fun-fair feel to it than showing signs of any real commercial recovery.

Genoa is eager to be rediscovered — but it hasn't been. It wants to keep the best of its chequered past and move on — but it doesn't. It wants to recollect and then progress — but it can't seem to do it. It wants to join the rest of the world — but it just can't bring itself to make the effort.

A bit like Italy itself, Genoa is in a bind. How much do you change without ceasing to be what you are, without sacrificing what you have already achieved, all for the sake of an indefinite future? You could theorise that this is a bit like the entire world really — failed totalitarian communism behind us, an uncharted age of politico-economic and hi-tech discovery ahead of us.

Genoa's Greatest Contribution — A Round Earth, America or Pesto?

'Come to Genoa with an open mind and a big appetite,' says writer Fred Plotkin. 'Even the city's detractors admit that the food here is divine.'

How right he is. It's all there in Genoa — authentic, fresh, out-of-the-wood-fired-oven foccacia; *torta pasqualina* with spinach, ricotta and eggs; *pansoti*, spinach ravioli with hazelnut sauce; and *trenette*, a local spaghetti with potato and pesto. And, as any self-respecting food-freak or culinary historian knows, the Genovese were the inventors of pesto, that glorious green paste of chopped basil, pine nuts, garlic, parmesan and extra virgin olive oil that these days is globally popular and goes so well with pasta of just about any shape. (In Genoa itself, we discovered, the pasta they prefer is *troffiette*, a flattish, chewy spiral.) Most of us have come to prepare our pesto with masses of garlic and pine nuts and finely grated parmesan cheese. Not in Genoa! In Genoa, pesto is thicker, greener and far more pungent, with only a hint of *aglio*, garlic, very few if any pine nuts and, more often than not, no parmesan.

The world has accepted Genovese pesto and changed it, not necessarily for the worst but changed it anyhow. But in Genoa, they still prepare it and eat it the same way they always have. I don't know if pesto was around in Columbus' day, but if it was, I'm sure he didn't smother it with cheese. He and his sailing mates from around the port would have enjoyed its oily greenness without adulteration.

A round earth we don't fall off, an America running roughshod over that same orb, or the lusciousness of pesto sauce? Which of these has been Genoa's greatest contribution to civilisation? It's a question you might care to ponder over a bowl of pasta al dente with whatever *sugo* takes your fancy. The sauce, by the way, is only ever there to coat the pasta — not drown and dominate it. Coating, not drowning or dominating? Now there's a more subtle political recipe the Americans might consider trying.

Equal Rights for Parsley — The Ultimate Italian Political Issue

When attempting to consciously interweave three outwardly stand-alone Italian cultural themes like football, food and politics, it's easy to get carried away with the whole idea. Nevertheless, in my view, the link is there, irrefutably. The real link is Italian life itself. After all, its three great cultural loves are *cucina*, *calcio* and *politica*. But a typical debate in the Italian national parliament a while back confirmed my suspicions. Food for political thought writ large.

In late April 1999, on the floor of the Lower House, Carlo Pace, a right-wing MP, delivered a passionate defence of the value of parsley to Italian cuisine. His speech was reported not, as it might have been, as a curiosity, but as legitimate news. Pace insisted that parsley or *prezzemolo* should have 'equal rights' to those other popular aromatic herbs, basil, sage and rosemary — all absolute essentials in Italian cooking.

Basilico, *salvia* and *rosmarino*, I was to discover, carried a VAT, or value-added tax, of 4 per cent. But poor old parsley copped a whopping 20 per cent. The reason for this discrepancy remains a mystery to me, even after considerable research in political and gastronomic circles.

'No one wants to eliminate the possibility of obtaining basil at a lower price to make pesto,' Pace said. 'But the truth is that basil can be found in any home. One can simply put a vase on the window sill.' True. That's exactly what we did in our own *piccolo appartamento* in San Giovanni Valdarno. No self-respecting family can be without a pot of basil somewhere and in small Italian apartments, as we all know, the window sill is the usual garden substitute!

Meanwhile, the blatant political discrimination against parsley took over parliament. An anguished Signor Pace pleaded with his fellow MPs: 'Why leave out parsley, which is used for every dish? I appeal to your gastronomical sensibility and invite you to look this situation in the face.'

'Or in the dish?' intervened the Speaker of the House, Luciano Violante, clearly a man of wit, if not a sense of equal rights for herbs.

Despite Pace's ardent plea, the parliamentary chamber voted against his motion by a thumping 248 votes to 42. Sometimes in Italy, it's a bit difficult to know whether the national preoccupation is food, football or the insane yet enthralling politics which dedicated but foolhardy types like Signor Pace are brave enough or mad enough to engage in — as is the case in many other parts of the world, I guess.

The Red Centre

In Bologna there is no need to even make a distinction between football, food and politics — particularly food and politics. Bologna *is* food and politics. Here, probably more than anywhere else in Italy, the three national preoccupations roll into one with amazing ease and fluidity, like a good *ragù*.

But it has to be said that Bologna, by some strange historical or anthropological quirk, is probably one of the very few Italian population centres where food and politics take precedence over football. This is not just because its red-and-blue-clad *squadra* has not performed all that brilliantly in recent years. In this beautiful, if little rundown city, politics, if you'll forgive the cliché, is food for thought and food invariably encourages political thought. Politics nourishes Bolognese intellectual and community life. If you're not interested in food, don't talk politics in Bologna. If you're not interested in politics, don't eat in Bologna! In this sophisticated Italian city, ideology is alive and well. It might have something to do with Bologna being one of those so-called 'university' towns that all countries seem to have one or two of, the sort of places that not only harbour but actually encourage different political and social thought. In Bologna's case, its university is said to be the oldest in Europe. On the other hand, the intellectual and political 'liveliness' of Bologna could also have something to do with the city being hailed as the country's 'food capital', the Lyon of Italy. Or maybe it could be a combination of the two. The city is often referred to as *La Dotta* — 'the learned' — yet it is also known as *La Grassa* — 'the fat'.

Jack Altman, a writer for Berlitz, speaks of the 'simple magic of the trattoria', those uniquely Italian family eateries, run by families for families. Altman reckons that 'the spice of life so treasured by Italians is there in abundance every meal time. From the unique punch of the early morning coffee via a steaming midday plate of basil-and-garlic-flavoured *tagliatelle al pesto* to a last shot of after-dinner grappa, eating and drinking here is always a heart-warming experience.' Spoken like a true devotee.

The Bolognese, of course, were the epicurean architects of the famous pasta sauce of the same unmistakable name. They, however, refer to it more pithily as *ragù*. Don't ever think of Bologna, however, as a one-dish town. As Altman writes, 'Its old specialities are now the mainstays of the national cuisine, but some things are just not as good as away from home': tortellini stuffed with minced pork, veal, chicken and cheese; *costolette alla bolognese*, veal cutlets in breadcrumbs with ham and cheese; mortadella sausage flavoured with white wine and coriander; and *bomba di riso*, pigeons cooked in risotto with their livers and giblets, tomato purée and parmesan.

But for inexplicable reasons — though ultimately fortunate ones — tourism has almost entirely bypassed Bologna. You would like to think that this semi-conscious oversight was not because of the overtly political nature and inclination of the Bolognese, but given the generally low level of interest, let alone involvement, in politics by non-Italians as a whole, it would not really be all that surprising if that turned out to be the reason, or at least a part of it.

Of late, Bologna has made a contribution to world politics that goes way beyond its stirring, traditionally left-of-centre local campus. Dr Romano Prodi, the Johnny-come-lately Italian politician jackknifed from the Italian prime ministership into the presidency of the EU after that organisation's notorious corruption and nepotism scandal, began his public life as an economics professor at Bologna University. Prodi, a gleeful, intellectually and politically pragmatic man, does not appear to be at all daunted by the rigours of his apparently thankless job. After all, he has Bologna, its café society, its splendid *centro*, its fabulous restaurants and inconsistent football team to come home to every weekend. What a city!

The Greatest Invention Ever — Beans or Soccer?

A few years ago, Brooklyn-based writer Paul Auster, along with a number of other notables, was asked by *The New York Times* and *Corriere della Sera* what he regarded as the best idea, invention or event of the last millennium. Auster responded without hesitation: 'Soccer!' Auster's reasons for such an emphatic choice were not given, but he evidently has plenty of empathy with Italians and Italian values, even though he has no known Italian roots or antecedents that I know of.

Soccer? He's got to be joking. Or is he? Is there a single idea, invention or event that has taken up more human time and effort, provided more exercise and pleasure, caused more heartache and pain, crossed more boundaries, ignored more religions or transcended more political ideologies than the world game? I doubt it.

In the same survey the Italian novelist and semiotician Umberto Eco summed up the last one thousand years of human endeavour with a different word — beans. Eco is one of Italy's more accomplished academic eccentrics, but *beans*? Explaining himself, Eco said he had considered nominating the aeroplane and the flush toilet as pinnacles of human achievement, but that the time had come to praise 'the humble legume', the one his fellow Italians call *fagioli*.

Eco's explanation for choosing the bean was characteristically complex and simple — very Italian, as I've already explained. It involved the bean's original cultivation, followed by an explosion, as it were, of churches, 'the concomitant introduction of crop rotation', the development of a new kind of yoke for draught animals, and the much-needed protein brought into people's diets. Via the bean, all of this, he reckoned, had helped repopulate Europe after the poverty of the Dark Ages. But his final comment was the clincher. 'Without beans,' he concluded, 'television would never have had a chance.' He's got me there, I'm afraid!

So what is it — beans or soccer?

Risotto and the Orgasmic Sigh

My real ambition was never to write books or appear on television. Strange as it may seem, my true and ultimate aim in life, still unfulfilled, is to become the best risotto cook in Australia. For a while risotto was regarded as one of Italy's best kept secrets, but in the past few years it has gone, as one recent article put it, 'from comfort food to gourmet delicacy'.

I actually already do a passable risotto. My culinary guinea pigs, usually family and friends — you wouldn't try out an experimental risotto on total strangers — often come back for seconds. Always a good sign! I'm sure they're not just being polite. But where risotto is concerned you can always do better. Platitudes about practice making perfect, or at least getting closer to it, really do apply. You don't just cook risotto, you literally have to *live* with it for the time that it takes to prepare it, which is normally around twenty minutes or so — momentary problems and monumental disasters notwithstanding.

What appears between these covers, of course, is not in any way, shape or form a recipe book, so I'm not going to give you my version of how to cook it. There are plenty of decent cookbooks around these days to do that. Indeed, one that caught my attention while researching this chapter was Valentina Harris' *Risotto! Risotto!*. According to Harris, making a good risotto is rather like making love: 'You have to be in tune with it and in the mood for what is going on; be receptive to all the little creaking, popping, crackling noises the rice will make when you toast it until almost singed. Then you breathe out with it when you finally add the first liquid and the rice rewards you with a hissing column of steam known as *il sospiro*, the sigh.'

Interesting analogy, but I don't know who Valentina's been making love to. Hissing columns of steam have not been among my lover's repertoire. Yet Harris is perfectly correct to compare making risotto to making love. I've often told interested inquirers that you don't stir a risotto, you fondle it, you stay with it, you keep coming back to it, tenderly stroking it towards its climax. If you don't pay it the right amount of attention, it will not respond the way you would like. And when the risotto has done its thing, then it's your turn. Fondled to perfection, it will then satisfy you.

But is there a political element to risotto?

From being a largely peasant dish that made use of whatever ingredients were at hand, the humble risotto has gone on to become a staple item on the menus of the world's most expensive and exclusive restaurants. Writes *Italy Daily* journalist Stefano Salimbeni, 'Like pasta, pizza and polenta, risotto is another example of how an Italian food that was originally for the poor has been turned into a delicacy.'

Italy, by the way, is the biggest rice producer in Europe, most of it grown in Lombardy and the north-west region of Piedmont. According to Salimbeni, of nearly 350000 hectares cultivated in Europe, close to half are between Milan and Turin. Similarly, of Europe's annual total of almost 2 million tonnes of rice, 1.33 million come from Italy. By contrast, Asia, the world's biggest rice-growing region, produces a massive 486 million tons a year.

Yet while the rest of us are clamouring for risotto, Italians themselves are not exactly ravenous rice-eaters. They eat an average of only 5.5 kilograms a year; northern Italians apparently consume eight to nine kilos a head, as against a mere two or three kilos in the South. 'In the Centre and the South, rice is often thought of as curing stomach aches,' says Roberto Magnaghi, the director-general of Ente Nationale Risi, a rice promotional institution linked to the Ministry of Agriculture. 'At best, it is seen as an outdated dish, associated with fatigue and poverty.'

So you see, the North-South debate lives on in a bowl of steaming risotto.

For Whom Does the Italian Bell Toll?

'Reject immediately,' writes Fred Plotkin, 'your notion of Italy as a country in which there is uniformity of taste, culture, language and history.'

Italy, of course, has only been unified, as such, for 131 years. Only in 1954 did the Italian Republic take on its present composition. Only in 1994 did the country's 'Second Republic' come into being, when existing proportional electoral laws gave way to quasi-majoritarian electoral laws.

In Italian, there is a word, *campanilismo*, that comes from the word *campanile*, bell tower. An Italian dictionary will tell you it means parochialism or 'parish pump politics'; in other words it means that Italians are intensely devoted to their own hometown, a bit like a dog urinating on a tree to mark out his territory, although you won't see Italians doing the same thing to bell towers, or at least I haven't! As Plotkin writes, 'Since practically every village in Italy has a church and a bell tower — whose chimes once told the time and dictated the rhythms of life in the town — one's point of reference seldom extended beyond hearing range of the bells.' Wherever you go in Italy, you meet *campaniliste*, people with this strong attachment. But ironically, Italians rarely profess any great sense of national pride — except when Italy's national football team is competing in or winning the World Cup. Or, to a lesser degree, when the entertainingly eccentric Roberto Benigni wins an Oscar!

The rest of the time, they're busy *competing* both regionally and locally, telling you how much better their local salame, pasta, cheese or wine is than the same products in the next town or village. Take the centuries-old rivalry between Parma and Reggio Emilia — less than thirty kilometres apart — over who makes the best cheese, ham and dried meats. Needless to say, this would-be gourmand has always preferred the famously hard and tasty Parmigiano. For starters, it's more expensive than Grana Padano, its counterpart from nearby Reggio, which has to mean something, right? Wrong! Price has nothing to do with it. In fact, Grana Padano makers claim their cheese is cheaper because their 'modernised but centuries-old approach to production and processing is more efficient'. But ultimately the question of who makes the best cheese has got far less to do with price and far more with tradition — and perhaps individual taste. In case you've been wondering, Grana Padano is milder than the more internationally sought-after Parmigiano, but its rind is just as rock hard. Of course, nothing political in this rivalry — is there?

Vino — The Great Loosener

The French might not like to hear this, but Italy has apparently been a great wine civilisation for something like 3000 years. So for that reason alone, among a lot of other good ones, you can't go on about Italian food without also talking about Italian wine.

To get a good grip on where wine fits into the Italian holy trinity of football, food and politics, I was told to seek out the Marchese (Marquis) Piero Antinori, a bloke whose family had been making and selling the stuff for more than 600 years since 1385.

Luckily, he was available to have a chat, and suggested lunch the following Tuesday at the family restaurant, Cantinetta Antinori, located inside the family palace Palazzo Antinori in the centre of Florence. What I had imagined would be a fairly dry, formal affair turned out to be an utterly absorbing three-hour feast with an elegant, worldly, amiable man with plenty to say about any subject I cared to raise. I started by asking the *marchese* why food and wine were so important to the Italians and how they were different from the rest of the world in this regard.

'Wine has always been part of our life. It's something that started thousands of years ago,' he said. 'It goes with the Italian culture. We Italians have always considered wine as part of our food — like bread, like pasta. That's why in Italy, wine has always been consumed with the meal. In the past, it was sometimes consumed outside the meal during the long periods when most Italians were working in agriculture. Until only forty or fifty years ago, farming in Italy was hard, physical work. And so one of the reasons for the very high consumption of wine was the fact that in the country, the workers used to drink it.

'They would always have a *fiasco* — a big straw bottle of wine — next to them and every couple of hours they would rest for five minutes and drink some wine to help against thirst, for refreshment, but also to get some energy. Wine was something that could give them energy instead of drinking just water, especially during the summer. One of the reasons, incidentally, for the *fiasco* with the straw was to keep the wine a bit cooler outside under the sun. They could also keep it wet to cool it a bit more. That's why they used to drink a lot of wine — for refreshment and energy.'

I asked the *marchese* how this straw-covered cask had come to share its name with a word that meant something very different in the English language. He laughed. 'I don't know why there is this coincidence. I don't know the origin of this use of the word *fiasco*.'

'Maybe it's because the word can mean something strange, different, unusual, almost a joke?' I said. 'In fact, outside of your country, Italy, it would be regarded as a "fiasco" to drink while you are working. But here in Italy, it appears to be the opposite.'

The *marchese* laughed again. 'Yes,' he replied. 'Quite the opposite. Anyway, the name of this bottle is *fiasco* and now it is a *fiasco* in the sense that it is not used anymore because it is very expensive and not very hygienic. Also now, work in the country is completely different. It is no longer so physical. We've got tractors and all sorts of machinery. As a matter of fact, in the last fifty years in Italy, we've gone from 25 per cent of the total working people working in the country to probably a figure of only 5 or 6 per cent. The Italian lifestyle has completely changed and that's also one of the reasons the total consumption of wine has gone down. These days, people are working much more in offices. They're not doing physical work anywhere near as much. We've become a far more white-collar country. Instead of going back home and having a family lunch every day like the past tradition, now people go to a bar and eat a sandwich. One of the results is that wine is now consumed much less than it used to be.

'But going back to your question,' he smiled, 'wine has always been considered part of the food of the meals and a way of socialising within the family. That's why even when the children in the family were very young, they were always allowed to have just a bit of wine. It was something to share in the family.

'One of the fundamental differences between Italians and other Latin countries is that they have always used wine as a normal drink. The northern countries have always used beer. Beer usually comes in a small can or a small bottle that you usually drink on your own. Instead, wine is normally in a bottle big enough that you have to share. If you think about it, it's a completely different social approach — much more convivial. Here, wine has always been considered like that ... I don't know if it's because Italians and some other Mediterranean countries are just more convivial and that's why they have developed this habit of sharing wine at the table with family or friends. Or maybe it's the opposite; the fact that they've always been using wine and the wine encourages them to become more convivial. I don't know.

'Here in Italy,' continued the *marchese*, 'it's very rare — including in the past when the consumption of wine was much higher — to see a drunk on the streets. These days, you can see people coming out of a nightclub on Saturday nights and maybe they can be drunk. But normally it is very difficult to see drunks, mainly because wine was not considered an alcoholic beverage.'

'The alcohol is incidental,' I said.

'It was incidental, plus the fact that it was used by

families as a convivial thing and also children were exposed to wine very young — not only because they used to see it but also because they used to drink it a little bit. In that way, I think Italians become more far responsible about wine as a product.'

'Then, of course, in countries where alcohol is forbidden until a certain age, maybe this encourages them to drink irresponsibly later when it's not forbidden any more — or even before it's no longer forbidden,' I said.

'Yes, but here because it's not forbidden young children get to try it, maybe mixed with water early on, maybe once a week, as a special thing. We don't consider it as the forbidden fruit.'

The *marchese* was terrific on this sort of stuff, but how could I steer him into discussion of the more overtly political?

'It strikes me,' I said, 'that whatever strata of Italian society you're dealing with, wine-drinking with food goes on, whereas in some other countries, the consumption of wine and alcohol differs greatly in type and quantity from strata to strata. But here in Italy, if you were in the South with a poor family they would almost certainly still have wine with their meals — the same as any wealthy merchant family, any wealthy commercial family, any wealthy professional family, or anything in between. Wine is part of the way of life, the way of eating and drinking regardless of your station or standing.'

'Absolutely,' he said. 'But also because wine in Italy has always been an inexpensive product, affordable by everybody — maybe even less expensive than some mineral waters! So it was something that was not considered a luxury product, but rather something like bread — basic food.'

Now we were getting closer to my favoured political thesis. I asked the *marchese* if that made wine a unifying factor, a social, even a political tool? Was wine something that automatically brought Italians together, despite their differences? Did the fact that all Italians were wine-drinkers help them to get on, even find political compromises? They're certainly pretty good at that.

He knew what I was up to and where I was taking the conversation. 'Yes, certainly. Wine is something that unifies. It certainly doesn't divide. In other words, you can hate somebody or have an argument or a difference with them, but then if you sit down at a table with them, with some food and a bottle of wine, often many problems can be solved in a friendly way.

'I used to say when the Berlin Wall was still dividing the world into East and West, communist and non-communist, with conflicts that seemed absolutely impossible to solve, that if the President of the United States and the President of the Soviet Union could sit down with a decent bottle of wine in front of them, maybe it would have been much easier to solve many problems we thought were unsolvable. Wine is something that can unify because it's something you enjoy with other people, usually when you're both eating. As I say, sit down at the same table with some food and a good bottle of wine and there's no doubt that something happens.'

'Is that why Italians have been able to overcome all sorts of political social and economic difficulties which would probably confound other nations? You do actually sit down with food and wine to try and sort things out. Or is that one of those international as distinct from urban myths?'

'It works with apparent fights within parties and between leaders of the different parties. I have personally seen, many times, political leaders who were huge enemies in the parliament or during those TV interviews, sitting in a restaurant or a trattoria, together, laughing about their differences. So I think that it helps. Most of the problems between Italian political parties or coalitions are solved over a drink. At the Parliament in Roma there's a *buvette* — a sort of bar — where they meet and maybe drink a glass of wine together. Most of the country's problems are solved there during a break in the Parliament, certainly with a glass of wine or something, and certainly at the tables of the trattorias around the Parliament in Roma.'

In most countries it would be quite the opposite. That sort of indolent, even indulgent behaviour would be condemned, possibly regarded as irresponsible. Sorting out political differences with a glass of wine in your hand. Outrageous!

Kirsty, clicking away with her camera, was into this wine-food-politics discussion herself. It seemed that in Italy the critical thing to do is to talk. 'But in America, for instance,' she said, 'it's more a case of how many hours you're in the office, whether you work back late and how often. Obviously Italy has as many if not more political differences than anyone — right-wing, left-wing, you name it. But somehow they manage to deal with these differences by talking, by communicating.'

That was the *marchese*'s cue: 'Wine is certainly something that helps people to relax and communicate better — whether it's politics or even business. In the US, they say the best deals have been made during a golf match or something like that. Here in Italy, it's more when people sit together, eating and sharing a bottle of wine.'

I returned to the subject of wine's ability to unite, to unify disparate social elements. 'In a way wine lubricates the entire Italian society, doesn't it? It loosens it up and makes people more acceptable to each other?'

'Yes, yes!' the *marchese* enthused. He was, after all, one of his country's most successful wine merchants. 'If Italy is like it is — with all its positive and negative aspects — I think that wine has influenced more the positive aspect than the negative. Wine has helped to socialise, to keep families together, because that also characterises Italy. Families continue to be something important, even when the old people continue to live with their children although they have young families themselves. In other countries they send their old people off to an old people's home or hospital, don't they? But here they remain in the family and if they're in good shape, they help because grandma can look after the children when the mother is probably working, because that is now very often the case — that married women work.'

It was fascinating to hear him argue so passionately that wine was a positive in Italian society. I told him that I found myself constantly being confronted by the paradoxical aspects of Italian society. Here he was saying that wine was a positive aspect of Italian life when in most other countries any alcoholic beverage is seen as a negative. We Australians put up with it because it's a reality that we can't avoid. It's part of our way of life. It's legal and all that, but we wish we didn't have to bear its destructive social problems. No one talks about it as a positive social and political thing.

Needless to say, I suspected the affable *marchese* had been down this track before. He had a ready response: 'Well, in Italy, that's really not the case. Wine has always been with us. You can start with the Bible, where wine is mentioned all the time as a good and positive thing. Then, if you read history, you see that wine has always been part of the life of kings, but also of ordinary people, the artists, the painters, the poets who — with some exceptions, of course — were always talking about wine: Roman times, throughout time, not just recent times. With so many artists, for instance, you always see a bottle of wine or people working in the vineyards in Renaissance and even pre-Renaissance paintings. So, as I say, wine is something that has really been an integral part of the history, even the culture and heritage of Italy. The Romans actually called it "the land of wine". In Italy, no one would say that wine is more negative than positive.'

So, for the urbane *marchese*, a man whose family has been involved in wine for twenty-six generations — which in itself is something to get your head around — was wine just a business?

'Wine is a business which is very special and very different from any other business — because it's not only business,' he said. 'And this is where the old traditions can help me, my three daughters [who all work in the Antinori company] and my father in his time. It's not the tradition in winemaking expertise, because that's a continuous evolution. Technology evolves, so tradition means nothing in that sense.

'But it means a lot in terms of love for the product, passion for the product. And that can be transferred from generation to generation. To have a long tradition helps in terms of the cultural assets — really the passion for the product and everything that surrounds the product, the vineyards, the cellars, everything.

'In general here in Italy, the wine business is considered something which you work for first of all because you have this passion for the product more than just wanting to make money out of it. That's necessary, but not the main objective.'

I could tell that the *marchese* — obviously not a screaming left-winger, nor a screaming anything else — was intrigued but not bothered by the political tone of our conversation. In fact, he was clearly enjoying it. He told me about the more direct political role of wine and food in Italy — for instance, the ARCI clubs. For the uninitiated, the ARCIs are local bars and *ristoranti* run by, irony of all ironies, the old Communist Party. I suggested to the Marchese that these sorts of clubs, with their good living, wine and food, would normally be the reserve of the ruling classes, the bourgeoisie.

He smiled: 'The ARCI movement, Arcigola, is led by a man with great charisma. I think his parents ran a *ristorante*. He really knows his food and wine. The ARCIs belong to the same political persuasion as Slow Food. They come from the same political origins as the old Communist ARCI movement. But that's not unusual.'

What the *marchese* seemed to be saying was that, in Italy, food and wine knew no ideological boundaries; they were their own ideology. 'Political leaders, including certainly left-of-centre leaders like Massimo D'Alema and the leaders of CIGL, Italy's largest trade union organisation, all have what he called "the same culture of food and wine".'

Over what was left of a splendid lunch — including a glass of the *marchese*'s Vin Santo *digestivo* with *cantucci di biscotto* — we proceeded to discuss everything from Bill Clinton and Mikhail Gorbachev, through to Roberto

Benigni kissing politicians, class warfare, bosses versus workers, how the Communist Party and the unions had been so successful that the Italian working class were now relatively well-off and didn't need the Communists anymore, and how much Italy had changed since the end of the Second World War. Four fruitful hours on food, politics and wine — which we now know, thanks to the Marchese Piero Antinori, is food anyway!

PART FOUR

POLITICS ON THE PIAZZA

'Everything is political! The bars are political, the supermarkets are political. The co-ops are owned by the Communist Party, but don't ask me which one!'

An Anonymous Tuscan Friend

Italy and Democracy — Marriage of Convenience or Group Sex?

You won't find the aforementioned question or the ones listed below in travel books or those dime a dozen memoirs that chronicle 'Why My Year in Italy Was More Frustrating Than Anybody Else's', but they're well worth asking. They are the sorts of questions that — even unanswered — tell you a great deal about the Italians and probably just as much about the rest of us. As a professional question-asker, I have often joked that the question is at least as important as the answer. Maybe even asking the right question is in itself the answer.

For instance, what is it about the Italians that makes them immune or antipathetic to the same political paradigms that we seemingly more politically stable and sophisticated types cling to almost pathologically? What is it about them — despite revolving-door governments and an apparent lack of commitment to any particular ideology or system — that allows them to survive and even prosper despite the twenty-first century obsession with globalisation and IT, which of necessity comes at the expense of individual societies and cultures. Why, over the decades, have so many Italian regional and city governments been of a socialist, even communist persuasion? Why, indeed, have socialism and communism never really been dirty words in Italy yet Italian national governments have long been dominated by right-wing Christian Democratic parties?

And on a less political, more psychocultural level, how can Italians have a worldwide reputation for being a disorganised, corrupt shambles, yet create fabulous fashion and design, fine wine, great food, fantastic football, and live in one of the world's most desirable travel and lifestyle destinations?

In short, how does Italy work? Why does Italy work?

I've been tackling these questions ever since my first innocent visit to Italy in the mid 1960s as a two-person-tent camper, that decade's equivalent of a backpacker. But now, something vaguely resembling an answer has begun to crystallise. Living in a foreign country is very different, far more revelatory, than merely passing through. The Italians might live to eat rather than eat to live, but there is no way they live to work. They work so they can live — to the full, *in tutto*!

The Perspective From Beach Umbrella 166

Midway through our 'Italian year', beach umbrella 166 at Francavilla al Mare on the Adriatic just south of Pescara in Abruzzo provided a rare opportunity for some relaxed summer reading, including a flick through the latest rib-tickler by American humorist P. J. O'Rourke.

A few years back, in Washington D.C., I met and interviewed O'Rourke. Over the years, he's made a name for himself by flying in the face of fashionable leftishness, promoting himself as the right-wingers' right-winger, the scourge of the American Left such as it is and of government, per se, just about anywhere in the world and of whatever political hue. Many among the pop culture set have seen P. J., the very funny, self-deprecatory crypto-reactionary, as a mirror image of that inimitable creator of 'gonzo journalism', Hunter S. Thompson.

Chatting with O'Rourke was a hoot. Having read his stuff over the years it had always been difficult to tell how much of his wild, Left-knocking view of the world was serious and how much of it was part of a routine. P. J., after all, writes for *Rolling Stone*, notorious for taking the piss with its cheeky, anti-establishment, rock-political view of the world. Face to face, I decided for the sake of argument — and there were a few — that the glib P. J. was at least partly an act, that many of his more outrageous opinions were largely a comedic construct. Some he probably honestly held, but others were clearly contrived for impact. The political basis for many of his views was so silly that I thought he couldn't possibly be serious. At least I hoped he wasn't.

But P. J. is an American. So many Americans, even the bright, incisive ones, seem to be convinced of both the domestic and global supremacy of their 'system'. They have to believe that it works better than any other system even though it's so patently flawed.

Years ago, one late night in a bar in San Francisco, an American friend confided to me that 'in America you are free to be anything you like, except that you have to be an American!' It's a comment that's rung loud and true ever since. Americans appear to have convinced themselves that the rest of us in the Western and non-Western worlds really want to be like them. They have no doubt that we are 'closet Americans' who secretly crave and covet their system. Yet not many Italians are closet Americans. Not the ones I met anyway.

As I enjoyed O'Rourke's *Eat the Rich* on the beach at Francavilla al Mare, between two-hourly dips in the Adriatic, going red, regular coffees, and playing *calcio* on the sand with the boys, P. J. not only raised a laugh or two — despite his tongue never leaving his chubby cheek — he also managed to canvas issues on the whole politico-economic scheme of things in the United States and the wider world. He had only one question to ask about economics: 'Why do some places prosper and thrive and others just suck?' And this response: 'I favoured the free market, not because I knew anything about markets, but because I live in a free (or nearly free) country and I'm a free man — as long as I call home frequently!' The Italians, I thought, would never toss off loaded terms like 'free country' and 'free man' in the same way an American would. To them, freedom is fragile and imperfect. It's relative. It has never been and never will be absolute. It's an ideal, a principle, a goal, an objective, a mechanism — not a tangible thing and definitely not a system.

Indeed, is there such a thing as absolute freedom? In whatever system we find ourselves — and over the last twenty-five years I have found myself in a few — hour by hour, day by day, we accept all sorts of big, small, highly significant and unimportant restrictions on our freedom. So much so, that more often than not, we don't even see them as restrictions. Rather, they're a bit of a bother — daily encumbrances and limitations set upon us by governments, by the law, the church, schools, business, even by ourselves. Maybe O'Rourke would be more justified if he claimed he might be freer than some but less free than others. If you're not convinced, ask America's tens of millions of poor, its drug addicts, its criminal subculture, its underclass of Afro-Americans and Hispanics what they think of American freedom. You will get a very different answer.

Surveyed, a majority of Americans invariably say they believe in God. Yet they must also believe in original sin, that some people don't *become* bad, hopeless or pathetic; they're just *born* that way! This 'blame the victim' mentality has always been rife in the United States. When people can't make it in the US, the O'Rourkes of this world would have us believe that the system is fine, it's just that the people aren't. On the other hand, when it suits, these same proponents of socio-economic Darwinism can tip their own argument a full 360 degrees. When the Soviet Union and the Eastern Bloc fell apart, they argued that the people there would have prospered if only the communist and socialist systems hadn't sucked! Hypocritical or just plain ignorant? My Italian friends kept telling me the Americans just don't get either politics or religion.

Get Your Priorities Right

In May 1999, Italy needed yet another President. No one could quite remember why it did, but party groupings and coalitions in the national parliament, from Prime Minister Massimo D'Alema's brittle but hardly democratic Left to Silvio Berlusconi's even less democratic 'Polo' Right, were having a ball arguing about who the next one should be. Yet while they were failing to reach a consensus on who should get the thoroughly unenviable job of controlling Italy's uncontrollables, its elected MPs, they unanimously agreed on one aspect of the election — its timing.

With one round left to play, it was crunch-time in the *stagione di calcio*. There were a number of games on the following weekend that could drastically affect the final outcome of the *campionata*, which, according to Italian priorities and principles, was at least as important a result as who presided over the Parliament.

With so much at stake, the 1010 pollies eligible to cast their votes for the country's presidency let the parliamentary organisers know — in no uncertain terms — that they did not want a clash between the ballot and the fixture in Florence between the league leaders, Lazio, and fourth-placed Fiorentina. This was the match that would decide if Lazio took out the championship. Similarly, the game between the Berlusconi-owned AC Milan and lowly Empoli was also critical to the overall championship result. A cross-party delegation was dispatched to meet with Luciano Violante, the Speaker of the Lower House, to beg him to broker a solution. Signor Violante agreed to their demands.

Without bothering to explain the mystery or the procedural intricacies of why there had to be four or five separate votes, *Corriere Della Sera* reported that if the election proved a thorny matter, as it had in the past, a vote might be held on Saturday while another ballot might be put off until the following week, giving time for political strategists to regroup.

But, as the paper also saliently pointed out, 'it would also allow Silvio Berlusconi, the Opposition Leader, to cheer for his beloved Milan team and Senator Vittorio Cecchi Gori to root for his team in Florence'. Needless to say, the critical vote was held on the Saturday night, before the vital Serie A matches. The next afternoon, in a cliffhanger finale, Fiorentina held Lazio to a 1–1 draw, ultimately depriving them of the championship. Milan beat Empoli, making them the champions, a result that pleased practically no one other than the few Milanese who don't support the northern city's second Serie A team, Inter, and, of course, Berlusconi. Who won the presidency? The broadly acceptable former Treasury Minister, Carlo Azeglio Ciampi. But I had to think about that one. Like most Italians, I too was beginning to get my priorities right. My honorary Tuscan family and I followed neither Milan or Lazio, but, of course, Fiorentina. It turned out Ciampi managed to get the numbers courtesy of an unprecedented but very 'Italian' accord between most of the country's major political parties. I don't know which Serie A team Ciampi supports, but off he went to the Quirinale Palazzo, the spendid presidential residence on top of the highest of Rome's famous seven hills.

In Italy there are not only ideas that are stronger than armies, there are, as we've seen, football matches that are far more important than matters of state, and not just the mere election of the nation's president. For instance, back in the spring of 1998, the Italian Parliament postponed a critical vote so MPs could watch the European Champions League Final between Juventus and Real Madrid. Later that same year, Parliament completely rescheduled its sitting hours to allow MPs to follow Italy's progress in the World Cup in France. Parliament only got back to normal — well, not quite normal — after the inconsistent *Azzurri* were knocked out in the quarter-finals after Luigi Di Biagio hit the bar in a penalty shootout against France.

It was the second consecutive time that Italy had been knocked out of the World Cup because of a bad miss in a nerve-racking penalty shootout. Significantly, there are no penalty shootouts in Serie A. Maybe the Parliament passed a law banning them? I'm only joking, of course, but in Italy they are more than capable of it.

As if twice were not enough, a year later the *Azzurri* again allowed the despised French to steal victory from the jaws of defeat in the heart-stopping final of Euro 2000. The entire nation went into a collective depression and the nation's politics came to a screeching halt. It took the country weeks to recover from the blow, which was far worse than, say, the collapse of the government. As the Italians display with dazzling regularity, they can and will replace a government. But they can't know when — or even if — they're going to get another crack at beating the French in a football final.

As I've said, it's all a matter of priorities.

Busted for Being Marxist

More or less at the same time that Italy's pollies were demonstrating that watching their favourite football team play was at least as vital as electing a new President, in the north-west of the country, politics and football were confirming yet again that in Italy you can't separate them for long. The confirmation came via a 'bust-up', as it were, between two smalltown Democratic Left mayors on the Italian Riviera. To really understand their classically provincial ruckus, an ideological reminder might be necessary. The then Prime Minister Massimo D'Alema's party, the Democratic Left, at that point in time the strongest in a shaky coalition government, is the reconstructed bit of the former Italian Communist Party. After the old monolithic Communist Party 'deconstructed', some bits of it 'reconstructed' into the Democratic Left while others didn't. They were still floating around the place in various post-communist guises causing trouble to themselves and each other.

The two warring Democratic Left mayors in question, Massimo Masini from Riccione and Signor Micucci of Cattolica, were also former Communists but had apparently not worked out exactly how they felt about each other in their reconstructed state. The result was that they became embroiled in a ding-dong battle over who owned a cherished bust of their very much fallen hero,

Karl Marx. It seems that this decent-sized fourteen-kilogram bronze bust had been donated to the town of Riccione by a private political club. For whatever set of reasons, around 1997 Riccione gave the Marx bust to the nearby village of Cattolica, whose town-fathers had stashed it in the local library. But then the good folk of Riccione decided, pretty much without warning, that they wanted old Karl back. The cranky mob over at Cattolica were having nothing of it, so Micucci came up with a very original idea on how the deadlock could be broken peacefully. Signor Micucci, would you believe, proposed a table soccer tournament between the two towns — indeed, between the two rival mayors. Masini dutifully accepted. 'I hadn't played in years, but how could I turn down the challenge?' he said.

For the uninitiated, table soccer, or *subbuteo*, is a popular game played quite seriously not just in Italy, but around the world. The fundamental talent required for what amounts to a mini-version of a soccer match is to finger-flick twenty-two small weighted plastic 'men' around a green gauze table top, the objective being to get them to 'kick' a tiny plastic soccer ball into equally tiny goals. Having played it as a kid, it's actually a lot of fun and requires more skill than you might think.

The crafty Micucci from Cattolica knew exactly what he was up to when he challenged Masini to a winner-take-all tournament. As things panned out, Micucci was not only a wily operator, he was apparently no slouch at the 'flicking' game. Both towns put playing squads together and in a week-long tournament that stretched to thirteen hard-fought rounds, Micucci and his Cattolica team defeated Masini's Riccione side 7–6.

The victors immediately announced plans to display the coveted bust of Comrade Karl next to another Marx work of art, this one a mosaic depicting the Marx Brothers, Groucho, Harpo and Chico, Micucci quipped, tongue-in-cheek. Only former Italian Communists could take the whole political reconstruction caper this far. Or as Karl Marx, borrowing from that marvellous line of Groucho's, might have said: 'I wouldn't want to belong to any Communist Party that would have me as a bust!'

Kosovo and *Calcio*

If football, *calcio*, is really as indispensable to the daily existence of the vast majority of Italians as it seems to be, how then can they separate the two in times of national or regional crisis? The answer is they don't try, as was amply demonstrated during the Kosovo crisis during the first half of 1999.

As NATO mounted its largely wishful airstrikes against Serbian targets and the conflict hotted up, the Italian media ran stories featuring reactions to the conflict from Serbian footballers playing in Serie A. At matches where they were playing, the fans, to their credit, somehow managed to separate the Serb players from the Milosevic regime and its oppression of the Kosovars. Not only that, many openly supported them in their concerns for their families back home. Placards draped from the stands and terraces assured them 'we know it's not your fault' and urged them to 'play on regardless'.

Meanwhile, the Italian Government's position on Kosovo, which seemed to say 'Sure, bomb Milosevic if you must, but also negotiate' on one hand and 'What about the plight of a million refugees?' on the other, was at odds with the likes of the far more hawkish Tony Blair and Bill Clinton, and made daily political life tricky for Prime Minister D'Alema. But it certainly made it easier for the blameless yet emotionally concerned handful of talented Serbian footballers playing in Italy.

Both on and off the field, there were no visible acts of protest or discrimination against them. For their part, the grateful footballers responded accordingly. The biggest star among the Serb footballers was Sinisa Mihajlovic, an outstanding defender with Lazio. The politically aware Mihajlovic was particularly vocal against NATO and was officially received by all of Italy's party leaders at Palazzo Chigi, the prime minister's headquarters in Rome. He thanked Italy for its conciliatory stance on the Kosovo conflict and took the opportunity to publicly lambast NATO's air strikes against Belgrade.

A week later, the fans were treated to what must be close to the ultimate in politics-sport mixes. It was possibly a trifle overdone and a touch theatrical, but an amazing mix nevertheless. And Mihajlovic, the not-so-reluctant *giocatore politico*, was again the central character. Playing in the annual and much-publicised derby between Lazio and AC Roma, the Serbian star found himself in a physical scrape with Roma's then striker Paulo Sergio. After some messy pushing and shoving, Mihajlovic received a red card from the *arbitro*, the referee, and was sent from the field — as was Sergio. Pretty normal weekend Italian football fare, one would have thought. Which it was, of course, but with a potent extra ingredient.

Soon after the event, Mihajlovic — a bit dour and not normally melodramatic about this sort of thing — blamed the red card and his sending-off on 'the bombardment of my country'. Belgrade, of course, is only an hour's drive and then an hour's flight from the Stadio Olimpico where he was playing. 'I cannot pretend that the daily bombing that is destroying my land doesn't affect me,' he said. 'When your head's so full of problems, you always end up making a mistake.' Hence his uncharacteristic onfield stoush with Sergio. Whether you believe him or not, it's unlikely you will ever hear a more extraordinary excuse for a professional footballer losing his block, getting red-carded and receiving his marching orders!

Better Dead Than Red — What a Joke!

The ideologically discerning Italians seem to be able to accept that there is more than one way to skin the political cat. The fact that their own political spectrum rages so wildly from the extreme Left to the extreme Right has always been evidence of this national characteristic. In the case of Sinisa Mihajlovic, most of them would have disagreed with Slobodan Milosevic's atrocious policies but accepted the Serbian footballer's concerns at the human level.

Apart from the years of almost endless carnage and catastrophic loss of human life, the so-called 'Balkans conflict' brought into sharp relief that old hackneyed adage 'it's better to be dead than red'. Could we in the West seriously suggest that the people of the former communist-governed Republic of Yugoslavia were 'better dead than red'? That was the ethical-cum-ideological question that few analysts and commentators, let alone politicians, were bold, honest or realistic enough to face. No matter what criteria you apply, the irrefutable answer has to be that there is no way on earth that it is 'better to be dead than red' — be it in the Balkans or anywhere else in this post-communist world. But don't, however, hold your precious breath waiting for this simple piece of high school logic to be acknowledged, particularly by the blindly right-wing ideologues of this world. The demise of the old Communist Bloc caused the mindless among the world's Right to leap about so excitedly that they could not, nor can they still, see the human trees for the political forest in places like the hapless Balkans.

If Western individuals and governments can set their knee-jerk prejudices aside for long enough to think back over the last post-communist decade, the facts outweigh any political argument in favour of the highly specious 'better dead than red' line. Under the hated former Communist regime in Belgrade, Serbs, Croats and Muslims were not annihilating each other in the name of ethnicity. For whatever set of reasons that did or did not relate to the oppressive nature of the old system, they lived in comparative peace. Back in 1994, at the height of the Bosnian mess, I wrote: 'They didn't get blown to bits standing in a bread queue. Their kids didn't lose limbs or lives as they sat in a classroom or kicked a ball around in the playground. They weren't cutting down their tree-lined avenues for firewood, dodging snipers as they queued for the one water tap left in the neighbourhood. They weren't burying their young in the backyard with monotonous regularity. Now they are and only one thing has changed. They lived under a communist regime before and now they don't. Is the freedom they now have — the freedom to kill each other — worth having?'

I doubt that there is anything else that better illustrates the philosophical truism that freedom is extremely relative than the situation in Bosnia. Whether the Bosnians are better or worse off is possibly the most telling moral question the modern world has had to face — at least since it was so eagerly propping up regimes run by right-wing military butchers in Latin America in the 1960s, 1970s and 1980s. The argument then was that they might have been a nasty bunch of political psychopaths, but they weren't all that bad. They were, after all, fervently anti-communist.

In the bad old Communist days, there was totalitarian rule in the Balkans, but there was no ethnic cleansing, no horror stories of serial pack rapes, no NATO bombing gaffes, no 'collateral damage', no gruesome front-page pictures of headless Albanians massacred by Serbs, and no endless streams of bedraggled Kosovar refugees, almost entirely old folks and women, dragging themselves and their children across the slush of mountain paths to whatever sanctuary they could safely find. Indeed, back then there was a Kosovo problem, but not a Kosovo crisis.

Democracy — High on Ideals, Low on Performance?

Those of us in the rest of the world's loosely defined, even more loosely practised Western 'democracies' have always enjoyed laughing at the Italians for going through more than fifty governments in the last fifty years. In fact, this superficially alarming statistic has long made Italy the butt of international jokes. But having lived among the

Italians for a while, I've realised that a discernible difference between our democracy and theirs is that they accept and have learned to live with political fickleness, indecision and inconsistency, while we continue to delude ourselves that we are stable, decisive, consistent and fair.

Maybe the Italians are the ultimate political pragmatists. Maybe they've worked out and, more importantly, accepted that democracy, for all its commendable and desirable qualities, is an ideal, not an answer. Why then should we be surprised, even shocked, when it doesn't perform to what are probably unrealistic expectations? If we are totally honest with ourselves, sometimes democracy works, sometimes it doesn't. Sometimes it solves human and societal problems. Sometimes, because of its inherent defects, it actually *creates* problems. It's the yin and yang thing again. And as usual, the Italians have the knack of embodying these paradoxes almost perfectly.

'Politically, we see ourselves living in anarchy in the land of paradise,' is how one Italian put it. Somehow, the Italians manage to be curiously egocentric, without being totally self-interested. They are unexpectedly philosophical, as their history shows in no uncertain terms. Political tightrope walkers, like democracy itself, fall off the high wire with almost monotonous regularity. But they have their safety nets, be it their religion, their sexuality, their food, their wine, their art, their music, their architecture, their culture or, of course, their ubiquitous *calcio*.

'We feel we must try to understand why certain things

happen only in Italy,' wrote Alfredo Pieroni in *Corriere della Sera*. 'Why, for example, is a new political party founded every week? Italians are acutely aware of the flimsiness, the makeshift nature of their body politic. They constantly knock themselves, their system and their institutions, perpetually fragile but simultaneously stubborn and durable. Why does Italy have so many parties? But if institutions are created by politicians, why don't ours create good ones? Maybe our politicians are too individualistic ...

'But it turns out that individualism is like cholesterol. There is a good kind and a bad kind! What we really have is a regime based more on anarchistic personalism. Italians are excellent workers. An unidentified Italian writer once said that the best recipe for transforming a desert island into a paradise was to put ten Italians there. But the same Italians joined together in a state managed to make Italy weak, disunited, poor and cowering. It's part of the same coin,' says Pieroni. 'What could we achieve if, for example, someone organised Italy's brilliant small enterprises? Or if our politicians united, rather than divided their vivid intelligence?'

South of Rome, They're Bloody Africans!

A few years ago, Kirsty and I were dining in our hometown of Bellingen on the mid north coast of New

South Wales with friends at the local ersatz Italian trattoria, a better-than-average establishment due to the fact that the chef was a Roman immigrant. Our fellow diners included a handsome couple from Italy travelling around Australia. Over dinner, with much pasta being washed down with ample amounts of *vino rosso* of the local variety, a spirited conversation about something to do with Italy took place.

To say the least, our Italian friends were enthusiastic participants. In fact, they were 'right into it', as we Australians might put it. They were arguing vociferously about a particular aspect of Italian politics — the details are not easy to recall — when Lucio shouted across the table to his partner, Adriana, 'What would you know? You're not even Italian. Look at the colour of your hair and your skin. You're an African! All of you lot south of Rome are bloody Africans!'

At the time, the significance of what seemed to be an unnecessarily hot-headed and bigoted remark escaped us. Now, with our Italian education continuing apace in situ, we understood a little better. Lucio was born and bred in Milan. Adriana was from Naples. Little more needs to be said! Indeed, when we got to Italy, we met northerners so openly prejudiced that they wisecracked that 'Garibaldi didn't unite Italy, he dismembered Africa'. 'Where does Italy actually start?' they would laugh. 'Rome, Orvieto or Florence? It depends how far north you live!'

If you thought that the political football that bounces non-stop around the Italian peninsula doesn't get lobbed from end-to-end between the wealthy North and the much poorer South, think again. And, needless to say, it takes a football yarn from Verona to prove the point.

Back in 1989, a match was being played by Verona at home against Napoli. As the story goes, the Verona stadium, packed mainly with fans of the local team, put on a particularly torrid demonstration of anti-Southern sentiment. As the visiting Neopolitans entered the playing arena, the Verona supporters broke into a raucous and rancorous chant of '*Terroni, terroni!*'

American journalist Paul Hofmann says that in the north of Italy, *terrone* is the standard putdown for any native of the South. Apparently, it's a derogatory word derived from *terra*, the soil. The term gets pretty close to the very non-Italian 'clodhopper', according to Hofmann. '*Terrone* suggests less a yokel than an uncivilised but cunning fellow with dirty habits,' he writes. He could even be lumped in with the *mafiosi*, while a *terrona*, to northerners, is 'a primitive woman who doesn't use soap'.

For the arrogant, self-satisfied natives of sophisticated northern cities such as Milan, Turin, Genoa, Venice and Bologna, *terronia*, the despised South, begins immediately south of Florence — hardly in the heel of Italy. The match at Verona not only encapsulated the North–South rivalry which borders on pure racism, but reaffirmed the gulf between the two when the locals hung from the bleachers huge barriers which read, 'Napoli! Welcome to Italy!' Four words that said it all.

The *Mezzogiorno* — The Afternoon Light and Shade of Italy

Italians from both the North and the South — for reasons that are sometimes even obscure to them — automatically refer to the southern half of Italy, that geographically distinctive spur, heel and toe that everyone everywhere knows so well, as the *mezzogiorno*.

Mezzogiorno literally translates as 'midday'. Why? No one I asked, not even southerners themselves, could tell me with any certainty. Whatever the explanation — and there is apparently no official one — there is an undeniable cut-off point where Italy *changes*. Where it occurs, of course, is open to question and depends on who you ask. The term *mezzogiorno* came about because at midday, the day begins its change from morning to afternoon, from daylight to eventide, from light to dark.

There are many, of course, who argue that Italy might as well be two countries. Some, such as the right-wing political party the Northern League, go so far as to suggest that the differences between the wealthy North and the poor South are so great that Italy should be partitioned. Without the

South hanging off its economic coattails, the North, they say, would be the richest place in Europe. 'This is probably true,' wrote the late John Haycraft in *Italian Labyrinth*, 'although they forget that much of their industry would have collapsed without Southern workers. Now, however, with the increased use of robots and the recession, Northern firms have survived only by reducing their labour force savagely; 90 per cent of the unemployed are Southerners.'

It's not hard to find detractors of the South, who mostly argue that it is only being kept alive by subsidies from the affluent and productive North. The government-inspired development corporation *Cassa per il Mezzogiorno* (Fund of the South) for instance, at one time Europe's biggest development fund, was spending enormous sums, tens of thousands of millions of dollars, on the four out of ten Italians living in the South.

Racism is also rampant in the North, and many Northerners refer to Southerners — predominantly poor agricultural workers more interested in secure jobs than economic enterprise like the adventurous, risk-taking Northerners — as earth people or peasants. 'Most shocking to a foreigner for whom racism is probably a dirty word is the openness and vehemence with which these views are expressed,' wrote Haycraft.

It is true that the North is twice as well off as the South. But it's also argued that the North has badly administered and neglected the South since it, to all intents and purposes, conquered the region back in the 1860s. Northerners, Haycraft and others have contended, are proud of working hard and are arrogant about their material gains. They find what they see as the slackness of the South difficult to accept.

Regionally, with its historic rivalries, excitingly divergent geographies, its array of culinary sensations and its myriad localised traditions, Italy has always been a wildly disparate place. There is a north of Italy and a south of Italy, and socio-economically, ne'er the twain shall meet. The stark differences in lifestyle, opportunities and material comforts between the North and South have paradoxically both changed and remained the same for centuries. Despite Italy's confounding ascension into the top five of the world's economic powers over the last twenty years, this apparent contradiction remains true today.

Over the past two decades, it has to be said that all-consuming and unpredictable market forces have done little to alter this endemic iniquity. The gaps remain yawning ones. If anything, they are widening.

One Culture, Two Economies

About ten kilometres outside the unsightly smoke-stacked port city of Taranto on the ball of Italy's foot, the rounded Adriatic Gulf between its wild Puglian heel and its even wilder Calabrian toe, the A14 *autostrada* from Pescara in Abruzzo suddenly stopped. It didn't just peter out like some highways do; it came to an unexpected and abrupt halt. As we'd finally learned to do after many aborted previous attempts, we shoved our *biglietto* into the automatic pay slot, quickly followed by our Amex card, and the sophistication of the North suddenly ceased to exist. No Customs, no Immigration. We passed into another part of the world — or at least Italy — not necessarily alien, but almost foreign. As we skirted around Taranto, its skyline dominated by the fumes and flames of the massive ILVA steel plant, Europe's biggest, through its shabby residential areas featuring those dreadful medium-density monstrosities that blight all Italian cities, it struck me that everything about the place was dilapidated.

The worn, poorly surfaced road was potholed, its grassy verge dry and brown. The normally immaculate planted flower beds on the side of the road were unpruned and straggly, the metal crash barriers twisted, rusted and sometimes even smashed. The cars — or at least the ones with Southern number plates — were unclean and knocked about, not just dinged a few times here and there as most Italian vehicles are. The road signs, not their usual crisp, neat, uniformly readable greens, blues and browns, were old and scrappy, some of them were close to indecipherable. One we drove past, passing through decrepit Manduria, was so battered we needed to turn around, go back and stop, twice, to be able to make out the place name and the correct direction.

Even our kids could see the difference. 'Wow! This place is poor. What's wrong with it?' they asked. We explained what the words 'unkempt,' 'neglect' and 'deprived' meant. They'd heard us tossing them around as we drove through outer Taranto. 'But why is it like this — so dirty and rundown?' our youngest son, Serge, asked. Out of the mouths of babes!

It was a good question. How do you tell a nine year old to ask the government? Ask the political scientists, the economists, the sociologists the historians, the Mafia, the corrupt Southern officials and the shonky developers from the North? Ask Rome? But, most cogently, ask those blinkered types who try to tell us that the North–South debate about the unevenness of wealth is over? Kids aren't blind. They can see glaring differences when they are right in front of them. Adults, on the other hand, don't see what they don't want to see and not just in Italy's starkly beautiful but impoverished South.

Even to fervent Italophiles, *gli ultras*, who bliss out about how Italy is probably the closest thing to heaven on earth, Tuscany in the North is one earthly world and Puglia in the South is an even more earthly one. Tuscans and Puglians both call themselves Italians. They both adore football, food and politics — three of the essential ingredients of *la dolce vita*. But that's where the similarities end. Italy is one culture, but it's two economies, not unlike the way the world is divided economically and socially between the northern and southern hemispheres. As we talked this through with the kids, we had serious difficulty explaining why Australia was in the south, but was basically rich, not poor.

In Italy's South, you are in the 'bottom' Mediterranean. It's dry, warm and sparse, decidedly unglamorous and non-metropolitan. It's part-European, part-North African, part-Hellenic, part-Levantine, even part-Middle Eastern. In out-of-the-way destinations like the inconspicuous rural town of Avetrana, half an hour from Taranto through flat farmland, these almost un-Italian characteristics were very apparent.

The flat-roofed domestic architecture had a manifestly Arabic quality. The streetlife felt and looked Middle Eastern, not as noisy, dusty and teeming, but Middle Eastern all the same. A sudden call to prayer would not have been surprising. Some of the occasional shattered *castelli*, castles, were distinctly Saracen. A dishevelled and pretty uninviting *ristorante* was actually called 'Il Bisantino'. As for *i trulli* — the bizarre cone-roofed stone buildings unique to Pugliese villages among the stony fields and vast olive groves inland from the rugged poor man's paradise of the Ionic coast — no one seems to know where they came from or why.

Bandy-legged old women walking on the side of the road were clothed in Southern mourning-black. Wine-ruddied, crumpled and unshaven, old men gathered on the footpaths outside their small, dark, cramped, two-roomed box-houses. In the late afternoon sun, they weren't drinking, smoking and chatting cheerily like they do in the North. They were just sitting, staring glumly, probably ruminating about what hadn't happened in their lives, not reflecting on what had. As Italian existences go, it was all pretty ordinary.

Yet Puglia, with its amazingly colourful history and engaging ethnic and cultural diversity, is an offshoot from the Italian norm. Invaders of just about every recorded religious shape, cultural form, military intent and colonial motivation raped and pillaged their way through Italy's semi-desolate heel. At one time or another, the Romans, the Greeks, the Turks, the Saracens, the Normans, the Spanish, the Levantines — virtually all of history's all-conquering Old World anti-heroes — passed through the place, leaving their culturally enriching calling cards. Like the neighbouring province of Basilicata, the interest shown in the region by the conquistadors of the past and now its neglect by its present overlords makes Puglia — maybe not as notorious as the likes of nearby Calabria, Campania and, of course, Sicily, across the narrow Strait of Messina — enormously intriguing. Don't ask me why the *Rough Guide to Italy* would have unsuspecting travellers believe that Puglia is 'still very much a province through which you pass on the way elsewhere, an echo of the Middle Ages when Crusaders stopped off on the way to the Holy Land'. Cute line, certainly rough enough, but maybe it misses the point.

Only a few hours' drive from the cosmopolitan chaos of cities like Naples and Rome, the desolation and remoteness of Puglia give it a 'Third World' look. Like Calabria — arid and stark, depressed but somehow economically resolute — it exemplifies just how disparate the modern world can be even within one country like Italy. Physically and culturally, Puglia is different because of its ancient invaders. Economically and socially it's different because of far more modern ones.

The Mafia

The greater South — Campania, Basilicata, Puglia and Sicily — has always been synonymous with Italian organised crime. Historically, the Sicilian-based Mafia, Calabria's 'ndrangheta and the Neapolitan Camorra make up Italy's three-pronged criminal brotherhood. Whichever colourful form of Italian banditry you choose, it is covered by the basic nomenclature *Cosa Nostra*, which loosely translates as 'our thing'.

As organised criminal activity goes, the Italian brand — with its jigsaw of political and religious ties, its multibillion-lira transnational network of extortion, prostitution and drug-trafficking, and more lately its infiltration of superficially lawful businesses both in Italy and abroad — has always been widely regarded as the most organised, ruthless and anti-social in the world. And not without good reason. Its record of assassinations, brutality and standover tactics is impossible to ignore. At one stage it was estimated that something like 60 per cent of all Italian business and political activity was under Mafia influence. Yet it is probably impossible to know exactly how influential the Mafia has been, how far its nefarious tentacles have extended. Is it merely the world's nastiest elaboration of business 'under the counter' or has it always had its homicidal hand on the tiller of Italy's entire socio-political and financial infrastructure? Have only a few Italians profited nicely from its heinous activities over the years or is it truly a nationwide case of *così fan tutti* — everyone being on the take?

As we moved around poor provinces like Puglia and Basilicata in the South, we found ourselves looking at the groups of retired old men innocently taking their breakfast *caffè* and *pasti* in places like Avetrana and wondering what they had done in their younger days. Had they demanded money with menaces from the friendly lady at the *panificio* where we bought our rolls? Had they been on the take from the *alimentari* where we got our daily *salame piccante*, *prosciutto crudo* and soft Southern *pecorino*? Did they still get their copies of *La Repubblica* for its left-wing politics and *La Gazzetta dello Sport* for the football results for free? Had they started building that horrible concrete mansion with the locked iron gates before the Mafia money dried up? What did that fat, ageing *caribiniere* know about them that we would never know? What were the secrets of their well-dressed window-shopping wives?

Just in case you had visions of the quaintly converted barn, the refurbished farmhouse or the rambling villa with its own vines and olive grove, this room was kitchen, laundry, living room and office. Most Italians live in cramped domestic surroundings; that's why they go to the football, to church, to open-air opera in the piazza, spend summer holidays at the beach and take the *passeggiata* up and down the *corso* every evening!

A young Italian spunk and an ageing Australian one at probably the best seafood eatery in the world, not far from Gallipoli, in the Puglian heel of the country. Italy's *mezzogiorno,* the South, might be poor but it's full of physical beauty and culinary surprises.

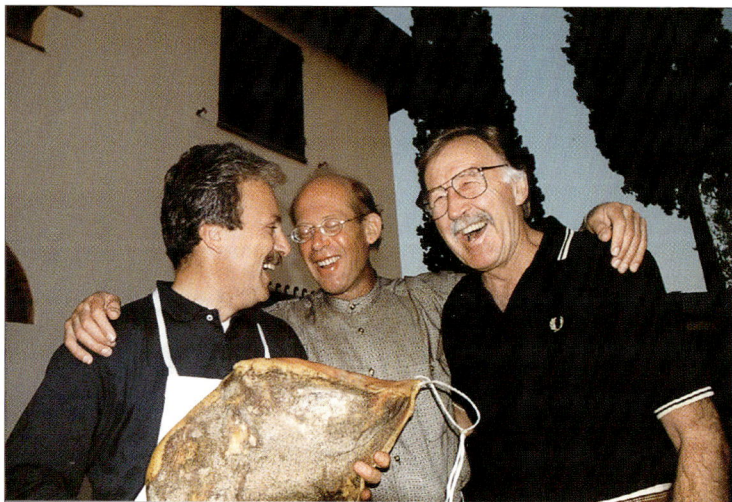

Stefano, our friend and favourite restaurateur, a visiting *Shine* man, and the author sharing a laugh and a shoulder of home-cured *prosciutto crudo* at Stefano's *locanda* at Cavriglia, in the hills outside San Giovanni Valdarno.

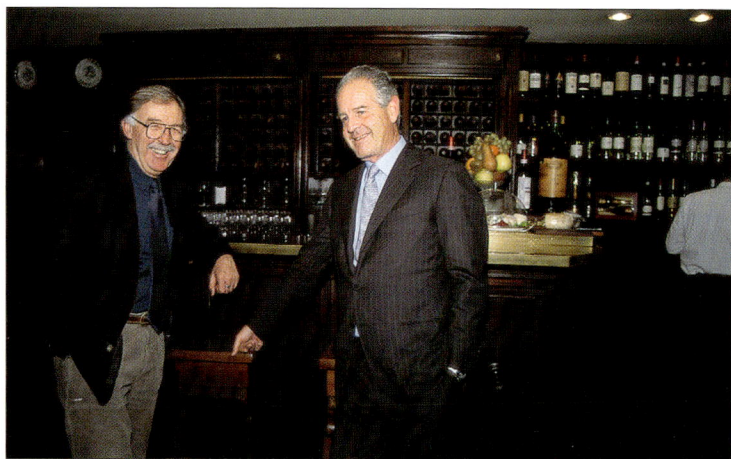

The Marchese Piero di Antinori, the urbane *patrone* of the country's most longstanding and esteemed wine family, told us that even the now-dismembered Communist Party has played a vital role in the gastronomy of Italian politics. The Party believed that tasty pasta sauces, fresh daily *mozzarella,* quaffable *vino rosso* and decent coffee should be affordable to Italy's working class and poor — so they opened Party-owned restaurants, *caffè* bars and supermarkets.

The best *macchiato* in whatever town we visited was often at the stand-up bar outside the local football stadium. San Giovanni Valdarno was no exception. If your first morning coffee is just right and your team wins, how can the day get any better?

Ice-skating in Firenze's Piazza Santa Croce — the last resting place of Ghiberti, Michelangelo, Galileo and Machiavelli, a notable Italian quartet, if ever there was one!

The San Giovanni Valdarno backyard of our relentlessly generous friends Lorella, Domiano and their three boys, Lorenzo, Tommaso and Francesco. But, as you can see, from the top floor of the two-bedroom house, to the summer holiday caravan, the Veedub on blocks, the ubiquitous shed and vegie garden, there's nothing that generous about Italian suburban living. Don't ask me why the Xmas tree is where it is.

This says it all about the South — tomatoes sun-drying by the sea. Not exactly hi-tech, and that's the best thing the South has going for it. They say that if the North and South of Italy were two countries — which they almost are anyway — the North would be the richest nation in Europe. But their sun-dried tomatoes would still come from the South!

Minus Kirsty, the snapper, one of our extended Italian families enjoys a simple dinner in the hills behind the Adriatic in Abruzzo — if 'simple' means *antipasto, bruschetta con aglio e olio, pasta,* seafood, heaps of chargrilled meat and vegetables, *dolci, vino bianco, vino rosso, pecorino* and *vin santo,* the dessert 'wine of the saints'. As they put it, the Italians live to eat; the rest of us eat to live!

What were (*left to right*) Tony Blair (UK), Fernando Cardoso (Brazil), Massimo D'Alema (Italy), Bill Clinton (USA), Lionel Jospin (France) and Gerhard Schroeder (Germany) — the major leaders of the Western world — doing in Florence's Palazzo Vecchio in November 1999? Here, 400 years earlier, Machiavelli penned that old political maxim 'the end justifies the means'. This wishful bunch were attempting to put flesh on the bones of the whole idea of a Third Way, the genesis of perhaps the first genuinely new political ideology since Karl Marx stumbled across communism.

The author in the Piazza Masaccio, watching the passing parade of Italian politics — or in the case of the old PCI, the Communist Party, merely the passing. But the Left will never die in Italy. Unlike so many in the so-called Western democracies, the Italians aren't shit-scared of ideology, let alone Left versus Right.

Tre ragazzi at Beach Umbrella Number 166, Francavilla al Mare. We'll be back
— for more sun, sand, football, food and politics. All the rest is mere detail!

Who would ever know the real truth? Unfortunately, virtually every pundit who's ever put pen to paper to write about Cosa Nostra has managed to make the scope of its criminal activities much more statistically awesome than it really is. Given the media's voracious appetite for sensationalist morsels, where does the bullshit end and truth and reality begin?

Don't get me wrong. The Italian Mafia is clearly an unlawful menace in every sense of the word, but it is also very much a by-product of the North–South divide.

Luigi Barzini, the much-read author of *The Italians* — these days a bit dated, but arguably still the best overview of postwar Italy — wrote that 'a man belonging to the Mafia does not know that he is doing wrong. This is approximately the way he sees things. Order has to be preserved. Justice must be assured. Unfortunately, men being what they are, it is often necessary to enforce the will of the Mafia by means of violence. At times, one is also unfortunately compelled to finance the operations of the law-enforcing *cosca* by means of extortion, robbery and blackmail. Do not many organisations fighting an unjust or foreign government do the same?'

Many would, of course, see Barzini's more sanguine, almost Robin Hood-like analysis of the Mafia as objectionable, even apologetic. It is not. If you bother to look at the history, the politics and the economics of the *mezzogiorno*, it's a very unfashionable, non-conformist explanation for the rise and existence of the Mafia, but not without its rationality. Unreasonable behaviour more often than not stems from unreasonable circumstances, Italian or otherwise.

In the case of the Mafia, it is not entirely coincidental that the world's most lucrative and successful protection racket emerged in Italy's South, where even today unemployment levels are two times greater than in the rest of the country. Mafias just don't happen. Simple farmers and small businessmen in obscure southern Italian towns like Plati and Corleone don't suddenly turn themselves into ruthless exploiters, standover men, drug-dealers, kidnappers and heartless killers. *Mafiosi* are not just born. They arise out of the ashes of their social, economic and political environment — or at least that of previous generations of southern Italians. They have certainly become both perpetrators and perpetuators of evil, but they are also victims of circumstance and decades of habit. The politics and economics of southern Italy did not make the rise of Cosa Nostra inevitable, but they did make it more likely.

The Third Way — A New Idea or Pasta Politics Reheated?

It may come as a surprise, but Tony Blair was not the first modern political practitioner to come up with the seemingly brand-spanking new post-communist, post-capitalist lurch to the ideological Centre that's been dubbed 'The Third Way'. Nor was it Bill Clinton's idea, or Lionel Jospin's or Gerhard Schroeder's. Not only did the politically much-maligned Italians think of it first, but horror of horrors, the Italian Communists did. They were tossing it around almost thirty years ago, long before the luckless Mikael Gorbachev came up with his previously unheard-of *perestroika* and *glasnost* and definitely well before the Berlin Wall came down.

John Haycraft reveals the shocking truth about the Third Way in *Italian Labyrinth*. The architect of *La Terza Via* was the benign left-winger Enrico Berlinguer, the longstanding and popular leader of the PCI, the then widely supported Italian Communist Party, the so-called 'Eurocommunists'. Berlinguer was what you might call a small-c communist, but he was no lover of Western capitalism, the US version of it in particular. Nor did he see any future in Soviet communism. In fact, he preached that the Bolshevik Revolution in Tsarist Russia in 1917 had outlived its validity as a model for both Eastern and Western Europe. 'We need a third way,' he told his fellow Italians, right across the country's political spectrum.

Old ideologies had to be dispensed with. Flexibility was essential, Berlinguer and his PCI colleagues said. While they stuck to the tenets of the State and central planning, they too had to be ideologically more open-minded. Not just the workers' needs had to be considered, but also the needs of management. They even seemed to accept what the cadres in Moscow and Beijing would have regarded as heresy — that private initiative could actually produce a surplus of capital which, in turn, could benefit workers, Italian or foreign.

It was radical stuff. What some of the world's leaders are now talking about thirty-five years later starts at very different points in history and on the ideological spectrum. Berlinguer was urging a movement from the Far Left to the Left. The 2001 Third Wayers are going from a soft Centre-Left position to somewhere in the indefinable middle.

Like a bunch of fossilised crypto-Marxist dopes, Italy's Eurocoms of the 1960s and 1970s clung stubbornly and counterproductively to the label 'Communist'. It wasn't until the latter half of the 1990s that the great communist carve-up occurred in Italy, including wholesale name and image changes for the various slivers of the multisplintered Left.

Would the Real Communist Please Put Up His Left Hand?

Massimo D'Alema was the embodiment of the post-communist era. He typified not just a quantum leap in the arena of Italian politics, but also on the European and world stages, where all the old certitudes had been thrown out the window. D'Alema was a near-perfect representation of a 'reconstructed Red', a former Marxist who had adopted the enemy's system and been adopted by it.

In the early 1990s, when the old Communist regimes in the old Soviet Union and its Eastern Bloc satellites fell apart, we were told that the world would move inexorably to the Right. It didn't, despite near-fanatical attempts by the single-minded free marketeers and greed merchants of the West to convince themselves and everyone else that it had or would. What actually occurred, in fact, was that the world — or at least large and significant chunks of it — certainly moved to the Right for a few short years. But then it steadied itself and, almost without exception, quietly shifted to the Centre-Left.

Britain's New Labour Party, under the super-pragmatist Tony Blair, and the Bill Clinton-led US Democrats epitomised this 'soft' Leftism. But it was D'Alema — the first former communist to lead a non-communist government in a country that had never been communist — who led this move away from the historic dogmatism of the Left. D'Alema not only reinvented himself, he was politically *reincarnated*, moving from comrade and cadre to politician and pragmatist.

A complex man, clever, eloquent, well-groomed, sartorial, cool, confident, media-savvy, appropriately coupled, in control and expansive, D'Alema was and is a paradox — a highly political one. In both Opposition and Government, he was politically agile, ideologically diverse, persistently effective, simultaneously autocrat and democrat, and, for a significant time, in power. However, despite this impressive combination of personal and political qualities and capabilities — qualities and capabilities that just about any politician in either the Western or non-Western worlds would kill for — he was a doomed man.

Displaying typically Italian flexibility, D'Alema was on *la Sinistra*, the Left, on *la Destra*, the Right, and in the Centre, *il Centro*, when it suited. But, most of the time he has occupied *il Centro Sinistra*, the Centre-Left.

When this wide-eyed scribe embarked on this investigation of the 'Italian perspective' of the international stage, D'Alema had been in power for just over six months. By April 2000 he had resigned, his brittle Coalition no longer sustainable after a crushing defeat in Italy's regional elections. But, in Italian terms, being in power for over a year was not a bad effort for any Italian Prime Minister, let alone a former Communist who had stolen the nation's top job from a popular and successful predecessor, the Centrist Dr Romano Prodi, by one lone vote.

Leading an unlikely coalition from the savagely divided Left and the hazy Centre, the reconstructed D'Alema had managed to weather a series of concerted attacks from Silvio Berlusconi's Opposition bloc, on Berlusconi's three television networks and in Parliament, which was very much unreconstructed and operating within an Italian electoral system that was also totally unreconstructed. Admittedly, his task had been made easier by the fact that Berlusconi was experiencing legal problems involving alleged tax evasion, dubious business dealings and blatant misuse of his private TV outlets. But on 17 April 2000, Berlusconi had the last laugh, his opposition coalition winning landslide victories in eight of the fifteen regional elections and amassing 50.7 per cent of the popular vote. D'Alema had no choice but to resign in order to avert an election which would almost certainly have been won by Berlusconi.

Yet while he was in power, D'Alema had his own very clear vision of Italy's future. On the one hand, he refused to demonise the global economy on the grounds that it would bring wealth and opportunity, but unlike so many of its devotees in the Right, he also recognised that globalisation brought with it injustice and chaos. D'Alema's view was that the undesirable by-products of the global economy should be countered by policies 'establishing a set of ground rules for the Italian economy'. With this dual-fisted approach to the so-called New Economy, it was no surprise that D'Alema became an integral part of the Third Way club — Blair, Clinton and Co — as their embryonic 'New Politics' began to emerge.

Florence — Elegant Host to a New Political Renaissance

The weekend of 20 November 1999 was an unusually big one for Florence. The self-annointed launching pad for the marvels of the Renaissance, Florence was again to become a launching pad, but this time for another marvel.

In town were the glamorous AC Fiorentina football team, the local heroes, who, in front of 40 000 fans at the Stadio Artemio Franchi, were expected to beat their less salubrious rivals from Perugia, another university city two hours south in Umbria, which they duly did. But across town, at the majestic Palazzo Vecchio, wedged between the Piazza della Signoria and the Galleria degli Uffizi, a smaller crowd was gathering for an event of even greater significance.

This event featured not *calciatori*, but vital players all the same in what was developing into the Western world's main political game — the Third Way. In fact, the international starting line-up of global political players was possibly without peer in the post-communist period: US President William Jefferson Clinton, British Prime Minister Tony Blair, French Prime Minister Lionel Jospin, German Chancellor Gerhard Schroeder, Brazilian President Fernando Henrique Cardoso, Portuguese Prime Minister Antonio Guterres, EC President Dr Romano Prodi and, of course, the gathering's genial host, Italy's then Prime Minister, Massimo D'Alema.

While Giovanni Trappatoni was in the dugout at the Stadio Artemio Franchi scheming his team to victory against Perugia, Bill Clinton, Tony Blair and representatives of the European Centre-Left were also scheming. But on this occasion, they were doing their political plotting not in the traditional 'smoke-filled rooms' but quite openly, surrounded by a throng of the world's media.

Not without its irony, the international political 'now-time' team were meeting in the same building where none other than Niccolo Machiavelli, the Italian statesman and master of political cunning, came up with his infamous maxims that guys like those gathered at the Palazzo Vecchio still subscribe to today. The quick-witted D'Alema had consciously invited this impressive collection of Western leaders to Machiavelli's city. Indeed, he had even arranged for his Third Way colleagues (the reconstructed Left would never use the old term 'comrades') to see the very office in which Machiavelli had worked on his pet theories. Machiavelli's most morally contentious and politically perilous assertion — wisely and unwisely exploited by politicians for 400 years since — was, of course, that in politics, 'the end justifies the means'.

The Florence meeting was not the first of its kind. Over the previous two years, there had been similar get-togethers, but this particular gathering in Florence had both the location and the portent to make it a genuine piece of history. It was a carefully planned gathering of the world's leaders, powerful men who saw themselves as the 'new progressives' in world politics. And the fact was, at the time at least, they had the numbers. In each case, their Centre-Left governments in their home countries were more or less unchallenged. Only Spain and out-of-sight, out-of-mind Australia were among the few Western democracies with right-of-centre governments possessed with the post-communist 'end of history' mentality. Indeed, leaders like Australia's John Howard and his Treasurer Peter Costello were policy-making as though Margaret Thatcher was still Prime Minister of Great Britain. Moreover, their approach to politico-economic matters seemed to suggest that the monetarist soulmate of the former 'Iron Lady', the arch economic rationalist Milton Friedman, was still dominating thinking in the US Treasury. The real post-communist world was in fact quite different. The bulk of the West had moved on.

Together and separately, the leaders gathered in Florence — all progressive political thinkers and practitioners from a broad ideological base — were coming to the conclusion that the demise of communism and its longtime bedfellow, undemocratic socialism, did not necessarily mean that the faults and failings of market-driven capitalism had magically dissipated. Rather, they had begun to look for something new. In Machiavellian terms, they needed something that would work economically and politically for both them and their electorate. They had discovered, as an Australian observer might say, that 'having a bob each way' from the Right and the Left was neither as silly or as outrageous as it might first appear. Maybe it would even work!

The possibility of a 'Third Way' seemed not so much ideological as just plain logical. As an alternative to the 'end of history' thesis, it had begun to make sense an increasing number of politicians, economists and social analysts — or at least to those not blinded by their own political insecurities and prejudices.

It has to be said that these self-proclaimed modern progressives were ahead of the public of their respective countries and indeed the Western media. Around the world, most people were still getting their tired, cynical, often anti-political minds around the fact that communism had slipped off into the ideological sunset. Either that or they had totally swallowed what disciples of globalisation and Silicon Valley IT evangelists had been preaching.

In the early 1990s, the battle of ideas had become pretty much a one-horse race. The undisputed winner was market-driven economics, whipped along by an irrevocable decrease in government activity and influence in the economy and even society as a whole. But this view was not shared by the big political hitters from the European and American 'soft' Centre. As a group of basically like-minded political souls, they didn't need much encouragement to accept D'Alema's irresistable invitation to spend a weekend in Florence, Machiavelli's think-tank, an appropriately old venue for unfashionably new ideas.

Their meeting hadn't even commenced before parallels with history, Italian history in particular, had been drawn. On the Saturday, as they streamed into town for their Summit, Steve Pagani of Reuters commented that the advice Machiavelli had given the ruling Medici family 'may echo in the frescoed Salone dei Cinquecento as today's leaders discuss their philosophy of how to combine policies of growth with social justice and yet survive the rigours of the ballot box'.

Growth with social justice? Was this a working definition of the Third Way? It sounded straightforward enough, but to pull off such a bold and untried political trick and stay in power, even these skilled survivors would need all the cunning of Machiavelli. The rampaging old Italian thinker put forward the idea that there are always ways for rulers to advance both their own interests and the interests of their states, via the amoral and opportunistic manipulation of other people. These days we call this sort of behaviour 'spin-doctoring'. So the Italians invented that too?

The New True Believers

Tony Blair and Bill Clinton were the real New True Believers. They were becoming increasingly convinced that there was a totally different political and economic rainbow out there and they wanted to lead the rest of the world to this 'pot of gold'. In the process, they were flying in the face of the world's post-communist orthodoxy. As Blair told *La Repubblica*, experience showed that markets as well as governments fail. 'That is why,' he said, 'we should not go back to the failed policies of the 1970s but work for stable macroeconomics and healthy public finances.' But Blair also warned against social democratic parties reneging on what he called 'their fundamental belief in fairness, social justice, freedom and equal opportunities'.

The Italians, the great compromisers, were of course up to their proverbial eyeballs in the whole Third Way idea, and groovy new 'soft' Leftists were in government in thirteen European countries. Their grip on European power had been loosened somewhat in places like Luxembourg, Belgium, Austria, Switzerland, the Netherlands and regional Germany, but nevertheless they were still the Western world's predominant political force. Some commentators had interpreted the backlash against the Centre-Left as a vote of opposition to the emerging Third Way. This was largely specious. The swing away from the Centre-Left was not attributable to any meteoric resurgence of the economic Right; it had been almost entirely due to brewing ultra-nationalism, neo-fascism, racism and xenophobia in various parts of Europe. Across the Atlantic, America's loony Right were advocating isolationism. The Republican-dominated US Senate had just shocked the civilised world by rejecting the Clinton administration's endorsement of the Nuclear Non-Proliferation Treaty — surely one of the most horrendous displays of abuse of minority power in Western post-Cold War politics.

But at the lavish pre-Summit dinner at Florence's spectacular Villa La Pietra, the New True Believers were not about to be daunted by distant domestic political travails. In a speech that received surprisingly little coverage at the time, Bill Clinton picked up immediately on the significance of the location and its history.

'First of all,' a suitably wine-relaxed Clinton said, 'it is entirely fitting that we're meeting here at this beautiful villa in this great city where the Italian Renaissance saw its greatest flowering. It's fitting because we instinctively know that we now have a chance at the turn of the Millennium to shape another extraordinary period of human progress and creativity. There are many parallels to the Renaissance era in this time, for at the dawn of the Renaissance, Italy was a place of great economic ferment and change, rapidly expanding trade, new forms of banking and finance, new technologies and new wealth, more education, vibrant culture, broader horizons. Today, we have the Internet, the global economy, exploding diversity within and across national lines, the simultaneous emergence of global cultural movements, breathtaking scientific advances in everything from the human genome to discoveries about black holes in the universe. We have, in addition, a much greater opportunity to spread the benefits of this renaissance more broadly than it could have been spread five hundred years ago.

'But there are also profound problems among and within nations. Making the most of our possibilities, giving all people a chance to seize them, minimising the dangers to our dreams, requires us to go beyond the competing models of Industrial Age politics. That's why we are here! We think ideas matter. We think it's a great challenge to marry our conceptions of social justice and equal opportunity with our commitment to globalisation.

'We will have to find what has often been called a "Third Way" — a way that requires governments to empower people with tools and conditions necessary for individuals, families, communities and nations to make the most of their human potential.'

Obviously warming to both the Tuscan wine and his theme, Clinton, the unabashed globalist, continued: 'There is no longer a clear dividing line between foreign and domestic policy. Therefore it is important that every nation and all like-minded people have a vision of the kind of world we're trying to build in the twenty-first century and what it will take to build that world. I think there is an emerging consensus ... about what works and what challenges remain. There is also a clearer consensus that no one has all the answers.'

This really was turning into a night of firsts. One, Clinton had used the loaded term 'Third Way'. It was official. Two, he acknowledged that someone other than himself might have something to contribute. On that note alone, this unique gathering of world leaders in Florence had already achieved a breakthrough in international relations! Must have been the carefully selected Chianti. The Marchese Pietro Antinori's special dessert wine was served at the Summit's sumptuous opening dinner. As he told me in his restaurant, Cantinetta Antinori, strange things happen when people, even politicians, sit down over a bottle of good wine!

The Third Way Balancing Act

When the serious business got underway, the agenda for the Summit was 'Progressive Governance in the 21st Century'.

With Clinton and Blair on the Right of the Left as it were, Lionel Jospin on the Left of the Right and the others somewhere in between, the Summit amounted to a coalition of principles rather than practice, of ideals rather than ideology. As one British journalist put it to Tony Blair before the Summit: 'Here we have an Italian Prime Minister who's an ex-Communist, a French Prime Minister who's proud to call himself a Socialist, yourself who doesn't use that word that often, and Bill Clinton who would never use it.' Blair's response, like Clinton's politically astonishing after-dinner speech, went a long way towards explaining the whole Third Way conundrum. 'It's a new type of politics for the Centre-Left, which is neither the old Left or the politics of the new Right. It's a renewed form of social democracy. There's a whole debate going on about how to have a market economy but not a market society.'

Market economy but not market society? It would come as a surprise to many economic rationalists that anyone these days — let alone a world leader — thought there was a difference!

The EU Room With an Italian View

While all this Third Way hoohah was going on, arguably one of the greatest experiments of history was taking place, a massive social, economic and cultural attempt to turn as many as twenty-odd separate competing nations into one single cohesive geopolitical entity — the EU, the European Union.

Fractious, drawn-out, strangely navigated, this potholed journey from a Europe to the EU has been going on in fits and starts for more than half a century. During that time and right up to now, it's had its ups and its downs, its enthusiastic advocates, its reluctant participants, its patient supporters and its strident critics. In fact, if you believe the more raucous among the so-called 'Euro-sceptics', the whole exercise has been one of the grand follies of the twentieth century. This far down the track, however, the EU is a reality — currently fifteen member nations representing 370 million Europeans. Basically, the vision is for a united Europe to operate as a single socio-economic unit with a common currency, but without destroying the individual national characteristics and cultural diversity of its member nations. It's an almighty task where success is elusive and hard to recognise. Failure is far more obvious.

To people like Australians, dislocated at the bottom of the world, the whole idea of a united, borderless Europe has always seemed a bit remote and fanciful and possibly even irrelevant. But given the enormous financial clout of Europe on the global markets as a unified, cooperative trading bloc, the rest of us, including if not particularly the Americans, will ignore Europe at our peril.

But in early 1999, before Dr Romano Prodi's appointment as EU President, the whole thing almost fell apart. A scandal over nepotism in EU appointments and contracts erupted. But it ultimately proved a blessing in disguise, providing a perfect excuse to clean up the EU and set about the business of democratising its lumbering, counter-productive bureaucracy and even its dubiously elected Parliament.

As I watched its beguiling political contortions from my Italian base, it struck me that whatever else it achieves, or fails to achieve, the whole debate over the EU, its role, even its very existence, has put the issue of government intervention firmly back on the agenda. The extent to which the EU should or shouldn't stick its nose into the affairs of its fifteen member nations is almost the counterweight argument not for or against marketism and globalisation, but to balance it.

Austrian journalist and writer Hans-Peter Martin, author of *The Global Trap*, sees the EU as providing the world with a human and economic force other than 'the dangerous world policeman', the United States. Martin is a fervent advocate of what he calls 'the European alternative', an appealing post-Cold War idea to anyone worried about the excesses of American economic and military power.

Like so many others, Martin reckons there is zero chance that the US would ever act 'to tame market forces for the benefit of every society in the world'. 'What is more likely,' he writes, 'is that US governments will increasingly turn to false protectionist solutions and seek to obtain other commercial advantages for their own country.' Martin fears that not only is the United States becoming more and more unpredictable as a self-styled, self-important global policeman, but that it is also failing in its duty as a guardian of world trade, something it professes to advocate and support.

The Europeans, Martin writes, must 'act together against this danger to counter destructive Anglo-American liberalism with a potent and viable European alternative'. Martin makes no bones about why this united-we-stand, divided-we-fall Europe is important — and not merely to Europe itself. 'A political union,' he says, 'joined together by a common currency and a painful but past history, would carry no less weight in world politics than the USA and the rising powers of China and India. In unfettered global capitalism, only a united Europe could push through new rules provided for a greater social balance and ecological restructuring.' This does not imply the creation of yet another 'over-weening European bureaucracy that regulates everything and everyone. Indeed, the opposite would be the case. Europe's recovery of the primacy of politics over economics would stop the hydra of bureaucratism from sprouting new heads.

'American politics, marked as it is by populism and demagogy, can hardly be expected to show the world a way out of the global trap. Nor is that [necessarily] a bad thing. The American refusal offers the nations of Europe a historic opportunity such as they have never had before. The EU could become a reality and its rulers could themselves take the helm of world economic policy in their hands.'

Meanwhile, in early 2001, the democratically dubious elevation of George W. Bush to the White House sent American politics rocketing into the 1950s. It also placed on hold any idea of a third political way being US-driven. The unworldly new leader of the world's most powerful nation has only used his passport three times, so he's not immediately identifiable as a Third Wayer. 'George Dubya's' way will be closer to 'God's way' than that of the politically progressive but philandering Bill Clinton. Can't imagine George Dubya relating his latest political thoughts — if he had any to start with — on Florence and the Italian Renaissance!

Needless to say, the Italian reaction to the whole Bush-Gore nonsense was great fun. Not exactly strangers to electoral fraud and confusion themselves, Italian headline writers lapped it up. 'It's Just Like Italy!' led *La Repubblica*.

'The US Banana Republic Election,' said *Corriere della Sera*. At the height of the absurdity of the electoral hiatus in Florida, one Italian commentator wrote, 'Dead men voting, missing ballot boxes, baffled voters? What's so strange about that? It happens here in Italy all the time. But at least we get a President at the end of the day!'

Not just the Italians, but Europeans generally, have always found the fundraising, spending and marketing of US politics difficult to take seriously. The 'great pregnant chad Presidential deadlock' confirmed their worst fears. Wait for their reaction the next time the Yanks decide to lecture anyone else around the globe about democracy — as they no doubt will!

Market Madness — Not in San Giovanni Valdarno

In the tranquil normality of life in a Tuscan town like San Giovanni Valdarno, forty kilometres south of Florence, off the tourist beat and away from the madding crowd, you don't have the freneticism of the so-called 'New Global Economy' in your face. The neighbourhood *alimentari*, the *focacceria* where we would buy the kids' *panini* for their lunch at school and take our morning *cappuccini*, the tiny *macelleria* where we bought our *salsicce* for lunch, and the *enoteca* where we would get our *vino locale* are all tiny family-owned and operated businesses and have been for generations. No one would have it any other way. Few, if any of the locals, would have heard the new jargon. Being 'online' to Massimo in the *focacceria* might mean taking a telephone call. Come to think of it, I'm not even sure there is a telephone in his shop. If there is, I never heard it ring during my hundred or more visits. It's another world from the one I found myself reading about almost daily while taking Massimo's marvellous *caffè*. The last high-tech thing Massimo did was buy a new state-of-the-art two-cup espresso machine! Point being, will the Massimos of San Giovanni Valdarno and the millions like him all over Italy and indeed the world, be wiped away by the forces of American-driven globalisation?

Their ultimate protection might well be being Italian — or better, European-Italians. It is hardly an international secret that the Italians have a strong commitment to family. But other Europeans have a sense of community too, much greater than the Americans. As Hans-Peter Martin points out, millions of European citizens in their workplaces, their neighbourhoods or in countless community, social and ecological initiatives, support alternatives of one kind or another that seek to preserve social cohesion in the face of what Martin brands 'world market madness'. As he writes: 'Many feel deeply uneasy at the very idea that the old continent might become more and more American. It is also certain that a huge majority of Europeans will not willingly follow the Anglo-American path of tearing their own society apart.' Even Italian automotive magnate Umberto Agnelli, the influential former head of Fiat SpA, has also been warning that if the social costs of adapting to the world market become unsustainable, a fortress mentality will again develop among EU nations.

Across the Atlantic, there are a growing number of doubters. Economist Ethan Kapstein, director of the Council for Foreign Relations in Washington, fears a human and social crisis may be developing: 'The world may be moving inexorably towards one of those tragic moments that will lead future historians to ask, why was nothing done in time? Were the economic and policy elites unaware of the profound disruption that economic and technological change were causing working men and women? What prevented them from taking the steps necessary to prevent a global social crisis?'

Bruce J. Schulman, a teacher of History and American Studies at Boston University, pointed out in the *Los Angeles Times* that a century ago Theodore Roosevelt said that democracy was in place to 'accommodate the interests of business', but that business must 'accommodate itself to democracy'. It was something, wrote Schulman, that still applied today.

That's probably what Bill Clinton himself was getting at in Florence, and you could hardly label Clinton as anti-globalisation, anti-market forces. Massimo D'Alema calls this push towards political and economic compromise 'The New Democratic Project'.

As Schulman wrote, 'In the age of the entrepreneur, it's a strange, uncertain new world.'

The Man Who Came Back From the Political Grave

You can't be in Italy and not be aware of the European Union. This ranges from EU flags fluttering beside the Italian tricolour, to price tags in Italian *supermercati* being in both lire and Euros, to the negative impact of uniform EU regulations on national food icons like homemade pasta sold at street stalls, to the dizzy rise and fall of the Euro itself. As only they can be, the Italians are both for and against the EU, but mainly they're for it, due mostly to one particularly high-profile Italian, Dr Romano Prodi. At one time or another an economics professor, businessman, Italian Prime Minister, MP, leader of the country's L'Ulivo or Olive Tree coalition (the Democratic Party of the Left), an overweight but enthusiastic bike-riding resident of Bologna, a typically fervent football fan, an Italian national and a European citizen, today he is President of the European Commission.

When I interviewed Prodi in Brussels, the Kosovo crisis was at its height, so it seemed appropriate to talk to him about the future of Europe. What follows are some edited highlights of our discussion.

GN: Is the job of European President harder or easier than you anticipated?

RP: Better, in the sense that it is really exciting. It's such a big challenge. Something like this has never happened before in world history — this idea of putting together so many countries, putting together a new currency. This is a historical event. And now [the EU] is trying to build a common foreign policy, some sort of common defence. The challenge is extending this political entity ... you cannot solve the Balkans problem unless you engage united Europe.

GN: Do you think that the Balkans crisis would not have degenerated to the disastrous state that it has had it been left to Europe to solve the problem; had Europe, in fact, been united enough to do it?

RP: No — because we have not yet built a structure to do that. But think it over. Europe was always destroyed by wars. But in the last two generations we have had no war. If you visit, say, Italy or France, you always see monuments to people killed in the First World War and the Second World War. It's such a huge list of names. Now, for the first time, we have had two generations in which no young European men have died in war. It has never happened before. Meanwhile, outside Europe, you have disaster!

GN: So do you believe that bringing countries like the former Yugoslavia, Bosnia and Macedonia into Europe will make the likes of the Balkans situation less likely to happen in the future?

RP: We have to adapt. It's a very difficult job. The intellectual scheme in which we stick together but at the same time preserve our roots is completely different from what is happening in, say, Australia or in the United States where people *converged*. They are completely new nations. Here in Europe, we preserve our roots, our history, but we are bringing together our separate sovereignties. This is a unique experiment in the history of mankind.

GN: Did you have these strong feelings about the need for a united Europe before this job was suggested to you?

RP: If I remember correctly, I was working on this idea when I was still a high school student … Italy is very different from the UK or other countries. After the war, we were a poor country in terms of income. The Italian income was only one-third of the British income. And now we have the same level of income. And all this change has been correlated with Europe. So you understand that old is more than what is new … I have also dedicated a lot of my intellectual attention to the idea of a united Europe — to the analysis of the economy, the European economy, mergers, acquisitions, European industry.

GN: Dr Prodi, do you see yourself as an Italian first and a European second, or a European first and an Italian second?

RP: It's not rhetoric if I say that now I feel probably more European than Italian ... now I feel that the future is building in Europe. This is the reality. Of course, I shall never forget to be Italian. I am Italian from my head to my feet, you know, with a passion, with the way I am acting. [Prodi was waving his arms about as he was talking, as only an Italian can!] Even if I become more European, you know, I shall never forget my roots. But our future is connected with Europe.

GN: Some would find it ironic that a former Prime Minister of one of the least stable democracies in Europe has been given this almighty task of stabilising the entire continent. Although by Italian standards you did remain in power for a long time, few would have expected an Italian to find himself in the position you're now in, heading up the European Commission.

RP: True. But this is the reason I feel so deeply responsible — because Italy has been a symbol of instability and even more because the Commission itself has had big problems with morality and so on and so on.

GN: People have suggested that the EU might be called the United States of Europe. Do you subscribe to that?

RP: Well, no, because it's not the same thing that the United States is. We're putting together people who have strong roots, a strong history, a strong identity, and you don't lose it, you know, going into Europe. But to sum up something new like this, you could call it the United States of Europe.

GN: Do you think that the argument about cultures being lost as a result of this union is nonsense?

RP: I think it is impossible. Maybe quite the opposite. Right now across Europe there is actually a surge of regionalism — flourishing, very strong regional autonomy.

GN: How do you feel about the fact that the whole EU concept, the Commission included, has become the butt of criticism from all over the world? It's criticised for being expensive, bureaucratic, for being a haven for has-been and lightweight politicians. Criticism has even been directed at you — that you are only here in Brussels because D'Alema and Berlusconi didn't want you around in Italy. Does this sort of continuing negative talk about the EU and the Commission bother you? Does it make it more difficult for you to do all the things you'd like to be able to do?

RP: Well, in times of crisis, I must be prepared to have all the criticism. Especially at this moment at which you have, must have, change in the EC. But you must turn the page of history. So everybody feels you will fail. But only time will tell the truth, you know.

GN: How much did losing the Prime Ministership of Italy upset you?

RP: [It doesn't hurt] anymore, of course.

GN: Not now?

RP: No, because I won the election. I put together a new political coalition. I invented it. We were treated as dropouts. I won the elections with a bus running through the country — with no money — against Berlusconi who is a tycoon. And then I was Prime Minister. The exercise was positive. I put Italy into the common currency. The balanced budget situation was better. We were rebuilding.

GN: Silly question, but if you had to make a choice between being Prime Minister of Italy or President of the European Commission — I know it's an invidious choice — which would you choose?

RP: The choices I have made. The first was to be the Italian Prime Minister, but now it's not. You can put rhetorical choices. Now, of course, the traditional parties in Italy have taken power again. So, for the moment, my experiment is put aside. It would have been impossible for any Italian to refuse this job — impossible, morally impossible because it's such a strong job.

GN: Going back to your own life, quite remarkably over the last few years, you've become a world figure. You were a figure in the academic world, you were a figure in the business world, but you are a relatively 'new boy' in politics. Did you have any idea in 1995, when you entered politics, that you might find yourself in this sort of situation — first of all Prime Minister of your own country and now in one of the most powerful positions in the world? Is that what you went into politics for, for power?

RP: No, I entered politics because there was a period of downgrading of my country. I was asked by my friends, let's do something. So, in order to put an end to the instability of the country, we built up a coalition [L'Uliva]. We tried to build some sort of bipolar democracy as you have in the UK. The idea was clear ... technically and intellectually we were correct, but in terms of power, no one gave us a penny. I was a loser at 100–1, you know. But I won!

GN: But nevertheless, in three short years we've seen the rise and fall and the rise again of Romano Prodi ...

RP: Well, I hope not to fall again.

GN: I've asked every official, politician and journalist that I've talked to here in Brussels this question and I'd be very interested in your reply. What do you think is the most important reason for the EU to exist?

RP: Ah, peace, peace, peace. You know what, when Europe was founded — and peace was in the mind of the founders — I don't know, they were full of blood. They fought terrible wars. Then, when the European army was defeated by the French, they downgraded it. Then they worked and created a structure, but it was second-best. The first idea was peace!

GN: And is that still the best reason for the EU's existence?

RP: After forty-five years, we've come back to the political reality of it.

One of the most amiable powermongers I have ever engaged, Dr Romano Prodi is the sort of politician you don't necessarily mind having all that power. Is it because he's Italian, because he's European, or because, despite what he is and does, he's also human — even normal?

Cybernomics — Spare Us!

One day, while watching Serge train in the freezing cold with his *squadra* of fellow nine year olds at the San Giovannese *calcio* club, I tried to keep my hands warm by scribbling some notes for this book. A few days before, our family had made the heroic decision to lash out on a new 3 million lire PC. The old one had been hopelessly inadequate, with the family emails, book-keeping and CD-ROM soccer games having to compete for hard-drive space with the folder entitled 'The World from Italy'. However, not long after the friendly installation man had packed up and gone, the whole thing crashed, leaving us to curse Italian small business, American big business, rip-offs, Bill Gates, and all the pluses and minuses that linked Italy with the global cyberindustry.

Our computer's malfunction had come hot on the heels of the history-making US$183 billion merger of the giant Time-Warner media corporation with the much smaller, loss-making Internet company, America Online. Europeans appeared particularly stunned by the sheer magnitude of the deal, the largest joint-takeover ever. As reported at the time, the combined value of Time-Warner and AOL represented something like 30 per cent of the GNP of Spain and only slightly less than that of Italy. European commentators bemoaned that while the Internet was driving America to unprecedented financial heights, Europe was being rapidly left behind with its policies aimed at protecting jobs by saving dying industries rather than creating new jobs in the industries of tomorrow.

The morning after the shock news of the merger, I was chatting, as had become pretty much my daily routine, with Pietro, who speaks much better *inglese* than my *italiano* and who runs the *giornale* stand at the *stazione* end of San Giovanni Valdarno's main *passeggiata* drag, Corso Italia. Like any Italian, Pietro has an opinion. However, he won't proffer it unless you specifically ask. But ask and you have to be prepared to listen to his reply — which in most cases is neither short nor simple.

'What do you think of this *grande* AOL-Time-Warner deal that's all over the papers at the moment, Pietro? Good or bad,' I asked as he passed over my daily *International Herald Tribune* and *La Gazzetta Dello Sport*, one in English for my benefit, the other printed on pink paper for better recognition in any language.

'*Grande, grande*,' he replied. 'Good or bad? Probably good for AOL and Time-Warner. But the rest of us — who knows?'

'They're saying that Europe — including Italy — is lagging seriously behind in the whole computer and Internet thing. What do you think?'

'Listen, we Europeans have been around a lot longer than the Americans. We're not stupid, you know. We've always been at the centre of things. We've seen all sorts of fads come and go. Wars, plagues, fashions, communism, capitalism — you name it, we've been through it. They've tried to tell us before that this or that was the answer to everything — and it never was. This could be the latest.'

'But they reckon you're going to miss the boat if you don't jump onto this Internet industry pretty quick.'

'Look,' he said, grinning in that marginally ironic Italian manner, 'just because we don't go mad for it straight away doesn't mean we're ignoring it. Let's see how it goes first. Let's see whether this American financial bubble bursts.

They can get carried away, you know. It could be a good thing — maybe not. But who do they think they are trying to scare us into computers we may not need.'

'But the Spaniards reckon it could already be too late,' I suggested. I had read a quote from the Spanish Prime Minister, Jose Maria Aznar, in which he said Europe had been 'left behind' by the United States in its support of high-tech industries.

'The Spaniards,' Pietro responded. 'What would they know? They're just a bunch of bullfighters who copped a fascist like Franco for years. They'll buy anything the Americans throw at them. No, the rest of us in Europe — except the Brits, of course — we haven't written off the whole computer thing; we're just taking a little longer to make up our minds. By the time we have, the whole thing might be a lot clearer. Europeans don't rush into things. As I say, we've been around a while and we just take our time over things. We play more of a waiting game. We've got a lot of tradition and culture — and mistakes too, mind you — behind us. The Americans haven't. That's why they tend to rush into fads and things and when they find out that maybe they were wrong, it's too late to stop and they have no choice but to keep going. I may be wrong, but maybe this whole computer thing could be like that?'

His words would prove prophetic, but I wanted him to keep going. 'I've always thought, you know, that you Europeans were the safety valve, the buffer zone between the Russians and the Yanks; that without you guys to keep them apart for forty years or more of the Cold War, they would have been lobbing nuclear weapons at each other across the Atlantic years ago.'

'You could be right,' Pietro replied. 'We probably did keep them apart.'

'Do you think that you might be playing that role again at the moment — acting as the buffer zone between the current American obsession with computers and the Internet and the rest of the world?'

'You could be right,' he said with that cheeky grin breaking out all over his face yet again. 'Guess you'll just have to hang around here in Italy for a while longer to see who wins — us Europeans or the Americans. We've outlasted them before.'

Totalitarianism Online

If you tried to tell most Italians that you were 100 per cent certain about anything — from the proverbial future of the human race to whether Fiorentina would win next weekend's Serie A match against Inter — quite correctly they would laugh at you. Perhaps we too should start laughing at the unswerving proponents of everything global, digital and online. They know that they are not necessarily right or even partly right, but meanwhile they are making mountains of money in the process of trying to convince the rest of us that they are.

Thankfully, in 2001, the fanaticism of the old totalitarian Left is behind us. That being the case, clearly, the next battle is to defend both commonsense and the practical politics of compromise against the new fanaticism of potentially totalitarian globalisation and the IT-driven information economy of 'Gatesism'.

This newest manifestation of the ratbag Right have set about urging the world to compliantly accept the raw forces of globalisation and multimedia technology. They would have us believe that they and their icons have all the answers. Their devotion to their commercial cause is far more like a blind-faith religion than a business model.

Fanaticism is fanaticism in whatever package it comes. The speaking-out bit of democracy is going to have to come into aggressive play if we are to contend with this *nouveau* religion that warns us we have no choice but to go 100 per cent global, to be online 100 per cent of the time, at the expense, we can only presume, of every other form of more human communication.

History being its own best judge, like always, somewhere between nought and 100 per cent will be the spot we should be aiming for on both these vital fronts, combined and separately. It is almost certainly where we will end up. So why do we need to go to extremes to get there?

As things stand, cyber-globalisation is looking and sounding a bit like Tolkien's *Lord of the Rings* — more about domination than benefit. The information control-freaks are getting a tad out of control. Larry Elliott in the *Guardian* pointed out that a few years back 'anybody who didn't sign up to the inexorably logical, efficient and scientific world that global capital served up was branded as one of the "stop the world I want to get off" brigade — and that was it. Frankly, this was always a ludicrous argument. If you're in a machine hurtling towards the edge of a precipice, of course you want to stop it and get off.'

It's hard to disagree with Elliott's commonsense rider that the ultimate question is whether or not, not necessarily now but down the track, globalisation 'can deliver on its promises or whether it is the sort of human, economic and environmental dead-end that the stop-the-world clan says it is'. As he says, the anti-WTO protests in Seattle in 1999 (and later, by association, in Melbourne in 2000) forced the supporters of globalisation into a crash rethink. 'For the first time in years, they have been obliged to find a positive justification for the way the world is heading, rather than simply repeat ad nauseum that there is no alternative.' But is Elliott correct when he claims that 'science is now viewed with mistrust, markets with contempt and globalisation with trepidation?'

Maybe, but many others have limply accepted technology, the markets and globalisation as a fait accompli. At this point, just a year into the new millennium, the numbers are indefinite, the debate is mostly vague and the results are largely inconclusive. My Italian friends say this is precisely how it should be. As a *vino*-sipping Tuscan *amico* with an opinion or two put it one day at the Bar Stadio: 'Sometimes the only way forward is back!'

Crisis, What Crisis?

As ridiculous as it sounds, it was the chairlifts making their immutable way up and down the snow-capped Plan de Corones high in the Trentino-Alto Adige zone of Italy's spectacular Dolomites that suddenly reminded me of that Italian paradox of all paradoxes. Like those unstoppable bloody chairlifts, the Italian Government is up one moment, down the next, but always there. When they do stop, havoc reigns momentarily — but only momentarily.

For a few days prior to Christmas 1999, while I was enjoying the warmth and comfort of the Residenza Frida in the *piccolo paese* of Rasun Anterselva, both the papers and the TV news repeated the headline word 'crisis' probably as often as our chalet's dinner menu included that hearty northern Italian standby, minestrone.

Yes, it was a crisis, but then it was over! Just like that. Probably to the extreme disappointment of Italy's millions of wildly gesticulating amateur political speechmakers, it only took forty-eight hours for Massimo D'Alema to be asked by President Carlo Azeglio Ciampi to cobble together D'Alema's second and Italy's fifty-eighth government since the Second World War.

As I sat in the alpine town's bar with my hands around a warming *caffè macchiato*, watching and waiting for the kids to finish their afternoon ski lesson, it struck me that like the people queuing at the chairlift, lots of people — some in highly unlikely groups, others solo or part of temporary groupings for the convenience — get on and off the Italian government with monotonous regularity.

Some of the passengers are bright and beautiful; others are dull and ugly. Some do it for appearances; others do it because they like it. Some see it as sport; others see it as art. For some, it's a lifelong commitment; others see it merely as a passing fancy. Some do it to impress people; others seek self-satisfaction. The way it works, both skiers and politicians usually join long, polite queues at the bottom of either the mountain or the pile. But when they reach the summit, things get less courteous as they scramble for a trouble-free run on the slippery, icy slopes. Meanwhile, the vehicles — the chairlifts and the government — remain pretty much the same. Only the faces, the fashions and the parties change each season.

To stretch the analogy further, the higher you go up the slope on the political ladder, the cooler the temperature gets. The higher you go, the more you need to protect yourself against natural elements and unnatural enemies. And when you finally make it to the top, the view is fantastic, the perspective is broader, the air more rarified. But the fall is much, much further and the landing much, much harder!

Clemente Mastella, the leader of the centrist Italian UDEUR (Union of Democrats for Europe) Party likens the role of the crisis in Italian politics to the 'liturgy in the Catholic church — it never changes'. Crisis, what crisis? Flexibility, what flexibility? Compromise, what compromise? One wise old Italian political stager, talking about his country's *Guinness Book of Records* entry for the most Western governments in the shortest time (fifty-eight in fifty-five years), offered me the following analogy for Italian politics and Italian governments. 'Same dough, different loaf!' he laughed.

PART FIVE

ALL THE REST IS
MERE DETAIL!

'Italy — the resonant subtleties of real places and imperfect people!'

Susan Cahill, *Desiring Italy*

Catholicism and Erotica — Italy's Secret Affair

'**W**e speak so much about sex!' is what Enzo Biagi said of his countrypeople in his pithily titled book *Italia*. Not only that, according to Biagi the Italian government 'officially recognises sex'. To back up this hefty claim, Biagi says that if an Italian lost an eye fighting for his country in war, he wouldn't get any compensation. On the other hand, if he lost both his testicles, he would receive a considerable sum in lire, around 100 000 back in 1984 when Biagi released *Italia*.

Seventeen years later, sex pervades the place — in the nicest possible way. There are a few grubby sex shops and the like to speak of, but it's just a part of normal healthy daily life like football, food and politics. For instance, any Italian schoolboy, for a dirt-cheap 1500 lire, or about US66 cents, half the price of a decent gelato, can pick up a handy pocket-sized magazine from his nearest *giornale* stand that supplies him with not just a guide to the week's football and TV sitcoms but

227

enough bare female flesh, photographically speaking, to keep him happy and satisfied long after the week is over.

In a nation most of us are used to thinking of as riddled with cover-all habits and walled sex-exclusion zones, near-naked female bodies are to be seen anywhere there's a magazine, a billboard, a cinema or a television screen. Just about every Italian television program, from sport and news to the myriad loony game shows in between, features phalanxes of stunning young, scantily dressed women aged between eighteen and twenty-eight, invariably accompanied by fat, ugly, untalented middle-aged men.

The girls don't actually do much; they're more like living, breathing wallpaper. Occasionally, some of them have minor speaking roles, but the majority are just there for decoration — flouncing, dancing, exposing their thighs and thrusting their main qualifications for the job, both of them, at the nearest camera. Last International Women's Day — an event considered by opinion leaders on both sides of the gender frontier as either totally irrelevant or a belated acknowledgment of something very basic and important — the 'gorgeous girls' of Italian TV were, unsurprisingly, the topic of animated media discussion. Donata Righetti in *Corriere della Sera* was especially aggressive. 'Why don't we ask for a real gift for all women and all men?' she asked. 'Why not ask television, both public and private, to suspend its panorama of pretty girls made to play the role of appetising idiots for one whole day?'

'Appetising idiots' was a phrase I wished I'd thought of first. It's terribly close to both the mark and the bone, except that it's doubtful all of those young Italian women in the Italian television spotlight are complete idiots. The days are long gone when the Gina Lollobrigidas and the Sophia Lorens of Italian filmdom were 'discovered' skipping barefooted and not-so-innocently down a cobbled village lane or sunbaking topless on a stony beach at Rimini.

It sounds almost as silly as these Italian TV girls can look, but there's something adolescent and harmless rather than sordid or soft-porn about it all — more like one long look-but-don't-touch lingerie ad. But it's also one of the more obvious mindbenders in this land of persistent paradox, sexual or otherwise.

The Italian Difference Between Alluring and Available

To outsiders, Italian sexiness seems almost innate. Most Italian woman have an allure about them. But their seductiveness is not restricted to lithe twenty eight year olds with long legs and flat tummies. Most Italian women have it — or at least think they do. For their part, most Italian men think Italian women have it — or at least want them to. Even today in this post-feminist era, you get the impression that Italian women have never needed liberation or never will be liberated. Whatever they are, liberated or unliberated, they are at once inhibited and uninhibited, repressed and aggressive, inviting and withholding. Another Italian paradox?

Take a quick, polite peek at any Italian woman under fifty and there will almost always be a glimpse of bare flesh, particularly in the hot months of the southern European summer. For four or five months of the Italian year, wearing less is not only sensuous, it's sensible. This is the season of boosted boobs, tanned thighs, uncovered shoulders, bared backs and acreages of cute exposed navels unencumbered by too much fabric. While Italian women pose, Italian men peer — both unapologetically. Non-Italian men, meanwhile, pretend not to look and non-Italian women pretend their men are not looking! But Italian women know that everyone is looking. One of the more telling comments I heard suggested that when an attractive young Italian woman looks a middle-aged man in the eye, he shouldn't get his hopes up. She is merely checking that he's looking at her!

Ogling is a national pastime, glamming-up the order of the day. Italian men are indubitably dapper and seem to stay that way even as advancing years encroach on the brashness of youth. It has to be said, however, that come middle age, that inescapable male leveller, the paunch, makes rather drastic alterations to the previously Adonis-like form of Italian men. For Italian women, there's a 'look' of glamour and sexiness for under-forties, but a more subdued, stylish version for over-forties. There has to be a *fattoria* somewhere remote in the South, like Basilicata, where every year hundreds of thousands of Italian women over forty are suddenly transformed from suburban sex goddesses into dumpy Mammas. This may sound like an unfortunate sexist male comment, but it's a cold hard Italian reality, especially in the poorer, more traditional South. Who does it to them? And why? Southern Italian women seem to accept that this is their sorry fate. All the same, all over the country, Italian sons never stop adoring their Mammas, long after the glint of desire has left their once-ardent *Papà*'s eye. Just ask their wives and/or girlfriends, who can spend an entire lifetime failing to live up to Mamma's standards in every way except in bed. The Oedipus complex, others call it. In Italy it's known as *mammismo*.

Only in the Heat of the Moment

At about the same time the Italian suburban sex goddess is transformed into the dumpy Mamma, a sizeable proportion of Italian men are transformed into much less than the perfect husband, the attentive lover and considerate partner.

As anyone who has braved it will tell you, driving in Italy is full of sociological surprises, including the one that lays bare, as it were, the popularity of drive-by sex. Throughout the peninsula from head to toe, on back roads and byways, in rain, hail or snow, Italian girls either too plump or too overtly sexy for Italian television, along with thousands of other young women literally dragged from Africa, can be seen *waiting*. They haven't missed their bus; they're waiting for some guy to spot at a hundred kilometres an hour what they have to offer. Business is brisk. After all, the appeal of prostitutes to these wayward men could probably be summed up thus: 'I've got something you want that she hasn't got and it will only cost you a week's wages — not a lifetime!' In the US, drive-by shootings kill people. In Italy, some sexologists argue that drive-by sex is possibly keeping half-dead marriages alive.

But Italian women cheat on their spouses too. Not only that, they do it more frequently, and are traditionally far more prone to straying than their male counterparts. A poll conducted by a popular Italian FM radio station found that of 2000 Italian women who went to the beach on summer vacation with their kids, but without their husbands, a whopping 29 per cent had 'indulged in an affair'. Among 2000 men who remained home alone, only 19 per cent strayed — that's close enough to one in three Italian women and one in five blokes. Remember, this is Italy, the same country British journalist Charles Richards reckoned the most common and popular form of extra-marital relationship was the *ménage à trois* — except that the third member was the remote control device essential for watching pornographic movies on the bedroom video player!

Meeting the Glam Post-Fascist, Post-Feminist Mussolini

Like any country, Italy is both enhanced and entranced by fascinating women. And Italy has its fair share of them — from the well-known to the completely obscure, from the young to the not-so-young, from the beautiful to the attractive for less obvious, non-physical reasons.

Lists are invidious things, but a considered group would have to include the likes of Emma Bonino from the Radical Party, who falls into the category of being attractive for less obvious reasons. The eloquent Bonino talks the talk about the danger of Italy and the world being swamped by IT mania. Then there is Cicciolina, the porn-star-cum-politician who became a mother (by American conceptual artist Jeff Koons) and subsequently fought for the custody of her child. Most Italians seem to accept her, despite disapproving of what she does. Also on the list would have to be Lilli Gruber, the heavy-smoking journalist from Balzano in the quasi-Austrian north of the country who became a household name as a television newsreader and then had a lip job; Carolina Morace, the one-time captain and now coach of the Italian women's soccer team, who scored more goals than any Italian male player, went on to coach Viterbese, a senior men's team, and got sacked for wanting, of all things, a woman as her assistant coach; and, of course, those redoubtable Italian icons Gina Lollobrigida and Sophia Loren, celluloid beauties of meagre backgrounds and considerable proportions with far more going for them than their ageless beauty. 'La Lollo' has even had a go at politics. Sophia is probably beyond them.

As well, there are friends we made in San Giovanni Valdarno, anonymous to all except their nearest and dearest: Maddelena, so young for her years, whose 'other Italian agenda' just doesn't exist; Rosella, flirtatiously close to being the 'new Italian woman' but with some very old Italian ideas; Lorella, so admirably together and considerate despite the trauma of almost losing her sick eldest son; and Anna Paula, the language *professoressa* and wise political animal whose English will be so helpful to her newborn son. Then there's our Florentine friend Simona, who wants so much to join her brother in Australia and open an authentic gelati chain there; our kids' teachers, open enough to see them adding something to the lives of the local *ragazzi* by their Australianness; and the local *calcio* Mammas, always splendidly turned-out no matter how early they have to turn up for the freezing winter morning matches. Italian women — we got to know some and talk to a lot of others. They were all worth knowing and most had something to say.

None more so than Alessandra Mussolini, the granddaughter of Italy's infamous wartime Fascist leader, Benito Mussolini. Aged thirty-six at the time of our meeting, the formidable Mussolini, the bleach-blonde former fashion model, skin-flick actress, nude *Playboy* model and unsuccessful would-be pop singer, is, at least by non-Italian standards, a trifle overglamorous. She is also a mother of two, daughter of a jazz trumpeter, niece of the incomparable Sophia Loren, and wife of a tax cop from the feared Guardia di Finanza. Just to smudge the bimbo tag, Mussolini also has a degree in paediatric medicine. But her public notoriety stems from the Il Duce connection. In 1992, aged only twenty-nine and running on an unambiguously right-wing platform just like her grandfather, Mussolini won a seat to represent her home town of Naples in the Italian Parliament. But after an initial blast of media attention and far-Right euphoria that saw her cast as a potential lightning rod for a pan-European neo-Fascist resurgence, outside of Italy not a great deal was heard from or about her for some years, except that she turned out to be more interesting and less blindly right-wing than most political commentators expected.

Early in 1999, however, 'The Mouth from the South', as the local media had dubbed her, burst back onto the scene. Appropriately attired in form-fitting blue denim jeans, she led women MPs from across Italy's wildly left-right spectrum in a protest that received worldwide media coverage. Mussolini and her coterie of high-profile 'new Italian women' were outraged by a court ruling that had overturned a lay-down misère rape conviction. A judge in Italy's Appeals Court argued that a twenty-two-year-old woman who claimed to have been assaulted and raped must have consented to sex with her alleged attacker because it was 'common knowledge that it is almost impossible to even partially remove jeans from a person without their co-operation'. Excuse me?

I met Alessandra Mussolini in the parliamentary rooms of her National Alliance Party in Rome. It was well worth the train trip from Florence. She had plenty to say about women, the law, politics, the rape case, Aunt Sophia and, of course, *Nonno*, Grandpa.

GN: People are very interested in you, your politics, and naturally your family background. But everything that I've read about you suggests that you are not the kind of politician people expected you to be. They expected you to be a far right-wing neo-Fascist. But now some say you are quite different from that description.

AM: Of course I am very different because I live in this period of history and in this society, so I'm fighting to change a part of society which is against women.

GN: But how closely should people identify you with your grandfather, Il Duce, because he was unapologetically Fascist?

AM: That is the past. My surname is, of course, Mussolini. Everybody knows about my aunt [Sophia Loren] and my grandfather.

GN: But to most people, the very name Mussolini conjures up the past. What's it like to be Alessandra Mussolini? Are you proud of it, ashamed of it?

AM: No! Let's say that when I was a girl I had two big stones around my neck — big stones like Sophia Loren and Benito Mussolini. Another girl, another woman may have said it is better to lock the doors and stay in the house. But I didn't. So for me, it's normal. Of course, when I say 'Alessandra Mussolini' I get a reaction. This helps me to know the person who is in front of me. I am against prejudice. You judge a person on what you think and on what she is. For me, Mussolini is family. I don't want to judge that historic period.

GN: How, though, would you compare your politics with your grandfather's politics?

AM: It's another thing. It's completely different. Everything is different these days. The mentality has to be changed.

GN: But people identify your grandfather with extremely right-wing Fascist politics. I guess what I'm asking is whether or not you see yourself that way? Is that your politics?

AM: I am in Alleanza Nazionale. It's a right-wing, let's say a Centre and Right party. Here in Italy we have the extreme Right, which is not Alleanza Nazionale.

GN: How do you feel though when so many people, Italians and others, judge your grandfather as harshly as they do?

AM: He's my grandfather. But you meet people in Italy who are still against him and people who, of course, love Benito Mussolini. We are in a free system.

GN: So Italians can say and feel whatever they think about him?

AM: Of course. If they judge me because of him. *Allora*, I say calm down, slow down!

GN: Has it been an advantage or a disadvantage to you, personally and politically, to be a Mussolini?

AM: It can be a disadvantage. How do you say it? A burden, a heavy load. But for me, it's normal.

GN: Normal to be a Mussolini?

AM: *Sì*, normal.

GN: It's become obvious that you feel very strongly about women's issues, particularly this recent rape case.

AM: Yes, of course.

GN: Why do you feel as strongly as you do?

AM: Because you fight when something is ultimately wrong, like this judgment on the jeans.

GN: You described this particular rape decision — the so-called 'jeans decision' — as a regressive thing that makes Italy look like a backward country.

AM: Yes, this judgment was a shame for Italy all over the world because nobody could understand this decision.

The judgment sends Italian women back to medieval times, the Middle Ages. It suggests that if you wear jeans or a short skirt, you're glad to be raped. Jeans or a skirt cannot be an *ostacolo*, an obstacle, to violence because a woman is free to wear jeans, to wear a skirt — to wear nothing, you know. Free not to be caught by a man.

GN: The judge seemed to be suggesting that a woman who wears jeans couldn't be raped, that she must have agreed to the man's advances?

AM: I do not know this judge. It does not matter if the woman wears jeans. If she is under a gun and a big man says do it, otherwise I will kill you, I would take away everything — not only the jeans!

GN: What does it say to you about Italian society that this sort of outrageous judgment could be made?

AM: I don't know. Maybe that it is an old mentality, that the judges are old themselves and they think that women are people who always submitted and bled sometimes. It is another mentality and I am fighting to change that mentality and the laws regarding rape and violence against women.

GN: Do you see yourself as 'the new Italian woman'?

AM: No — I'm a woman. I'm Italian and I'm like other women that are working in offices. I am fighting in the Parliament for them and for myself too, because I have two children.

GN: Two girls?

AM: Two girls, very little. I have to fight for them because I want them to live in a society where they can wear what they like, you know?

GN: You've described what you are involved in as a war.

AM: It's a fight against the laws, the Supreme Court, the magistrates and the political institution of the Parliament.

GN: Women are not reporting rape?

AM: Because they are afraid and this is very dangerous.

GN: And you have also been very outspoken on other sexual issues such as paedophilia, homosexuality and fertility.

AM: *Sì!*

GN: How do the other members of your National Alliance Party feel about this? Because it is a very socially conservative party.

AM: Very stimulated! They actually get very excited by my ideas. I am what I am.

GN: But do they like your ideas?

AM: They like and they don't like.

GN: Is it the right party for you?

AM: Yes, I think so. I am free to express my ideas, so for me it's the right party — right Right!

GN: But quite often you've had serious differences of opinion with your leader, Gianfranco Fini.

AM: Of course, when you are working in the social field, you cannot make a law that suits everyone, Left or Right. It's not a party matter.

GN: But do your party colleagues and your leader say, 'Look, Alessandra, please be a little quieter, a little more conservative on these issues'?

AM: Ah, Alessandra cannot be quiet! I am fighting for women wherever they are, even at home where they work and don't get paid. That's the case, I think, all over — even in Australia.

GN: Do you think that people take you seriously as a politician?

AM: I hope so. You can't know for sure. Who knows?

GN: Do you have a double problem, being not just your notorious family background, but also being a woman?

AM: Why don't you ask this question of D'Alema? He has children. Prodi and Fini have children.

GN: But your political opponents have also used your appearance as a weapon against you.

AM: But when you're positive about it, it can be a positive. If you are a *pessimista*, a pessimist, everything is wrong.

GN: You could say that it's okay for unattractive men to be in politics, but it's not okay for attractive women to be in politics.

AM: Attractive? Hah! That's another problem! I don't think a woman should be judged on whether or not she is attractive. What is good-looking? Men also want to be attractive and they use the same seduction [techniques] as women.

GN: So, as you see it, it's part of the overall discrimination against women?

AM: *Sì! Sì! Sì! Maschilista!* Let's say that your questions are a little bit *maschilista* — just a little!

GN: I hope only a little. No, I asked the question because people have said these things about an attractive woman like yourself being in politics, not because I am necessarily prejudiced.

AM: If a woman is judged to be good-looking, it can help as well . . .

GN: Is there one thing that you would like to do that you will be remembered for, rather than for your family background?

AM: When people know me or they meet me they recognise me as a woman who fights for good things, for social things. I am not involved in strategic politics, party politics. That's the politics that I don't like.

GN: When you protested against the 'jeans decision' in that rape case, women from right across Italy's political spectrum joined you. What does that say?

AM: It means that it was not a party matter. On the Left or the Right, they said Alessandra go on. This is wrong. They said that from Left to Right to Centre.

GN: So there are some issues — like this one of rape — that cut right across party lines?

AM: *Sì!* And not just parties. From all over they called me — even from places like Saudi Arabia! This judgment was a shame for us, but there it's an even bigger problem.

GN: Are you going to continue in politics?

AM: You continue if you are voted in. That is democracy.

GN: But there have been suggestions that maybe you were not — as we say in English — in for the long haul, for a long period.

AM: Of course I am. This is my life now. I would not change it.

GN: Can you combine being a politician with being a mother? That's another very big women's issue.

AM: Women have this role — to do both. I have no private life because I go to bed at 8.30 p.m. I get up early with my young daughters. I do my work like other women.

GN: When you went into acting years ago, your aunt, Sophia Loren, said she was pleased that someone else in the family was becoming an actress. But what does she think about you being in politics?

AM: She's actually very, very happy — first of all because of this thing of the jeans. She called me and said, 'Alessandra, what are you going to do?' because everybody was talking about this sentence.

GN: She was supportive? She agreed with you?

AM: *Sì, sì, sì, sì!*

GN: This may seem like a silly question, but if you had a choice between being Benito Mussolini's granddaughter and Sophia Loren's niece, what would you choose?

AM: I cannot answer because I'm a mix — an explosive mix!

GN: An explosive mix?

AM: Yes, of the two together. So I am half-North, because my father is Roman and my mother is not Neapolitan, but a little bit further South. So, I'm a mix.

GN: Does it get tiring to be answering questions about being a Mussolini?

AM: *Sì*. I am very tired of it because, when you think about it, is it a problem for me to have that last name or is it a problem for others? I think it is more of a problem for others.

GN: Have you ever thought of changing your name?

AM: Why change it? It is me. I don't want to hide myself, my family, because I'm proud of my family. I am happy with my family. It's normal. If you change your last name, it's not you, it's a mask and then people would say you are wearing a mask. It's not you. Can you wear a mask all your life? I think it is impossible.

It's All in the Italian Family

The Mussolinis are hardly your average Italian family, but if you want to see Italian family life as it's really lived, go to the beach — almost any Italian beach — in June, July or August: school holiday time. For those three months, the beaches are wall-to-wall or rather brolly-to-brolly Italian families.

They arrive at nine in the morning together, sit together, swim together, play cards together, snooze together, tan together, stroll together, take *caffè* and *gelati* at the beach bar together, eat *panini* together, drink *vino locale* together. They kick soccer balls around together, bounce up and down and swivel their hips knee-deep at aquarobics together, belt tennis balls back and forth with wooden bats together. They wade out to the man-made groynes together and collect shells together. The men ogle together at the young girls in string bikinis. Their wives and girlfriends who happen to wear equally revealing versions, glare together at their men ogling the young girls in string bikinis. At around seven or eight each evening, when the sting has gone out of the sun, they wander off together, pack the Fiat together and go home together.

The next day and the next and the next, they do this together all over again until their summer holidays are over. Then they go back home to whatever city, town or village they come from together and do whatever they do there together. The next year and the next and the next, they'll do exactly the same things all over again — together!

In short, Italian life is *togetherness*. Or at least it was until quite recently. Even so, maybe the Italians' affinity with family life is why they always seem so contented, at ease with the simplicity, predictability and domesticity of all this togetherness. It might border on triteness, but there seems to be a pervading Italian attitude that life can always be better but it's a lot easier to live with its deficiencies if you're reasonably satisfied with what you've got. This is not to say that Italy is necessarily all that egalitarian or classless. Far from it. There are clear and identifiable social and monied classes in Italy. But most Italians live a totally different existence from one predicated on income and status. Houses may be larger, cars faster, clothes designer-swankier, the kids cleaner, but the pasta is no hotter, the sauce is no tastier, the wine is no less soothing. Whatever the class or socio-economic status, *caffè* and *pasti* in the morning is still a clockwork habit, while Mass is irregularly attended and the local football team's fortunes are religiously followed.

On the *lungomare* at Francavilla al Mare, on the grey, gritty sand under beach umbrella 166 with our two deck chairs and canvas lounge, I couldn't tell the socio-economic standing of our fellow family holidaymakers. They could have been well-off; they could have been badly off. Their kids still played with the same cheap plastic buckets, spades and nets and wore the same waterproof rubber shoes. They all left the beach at one to go somewhere, maybe home, maybe not, for lunch and returned at four. I don't know exactly what they did during the bizarre, nationally-adhered-to three-hour afternoon siesta when all of Italy goes eerily quiet, but it was probably the same sort of eat-and-sleep routine for all of them. Is this the Italian answer to egalitarianism or just Italian lack of imagination? Either way, they all do it and appear to like doing it. No doubt, they will keep doing it. They're Italian! These are the things that Italians do.

The Octogenarian Scientist and the Supermodel

Speaking of things Italians do, according to eighty-nine-year-old Indro Montanelli, Italians like nothing more than watching the San Remo Festival, the country's most popular television special. Only San Remo, and the Italians, could feature Lucianno Pavorotti and Sting on the same bill. When the 1999 telecast of this annual songfest up in the north-west near the border with the French Riviera scored massive viewer ratings on its final night, an onstage meeting of the unlikeliest sort typified the almost bottomless Italian propensity for contrast and contradiction. The two hosts of the program were twenty-year-old supermodel Laetitia Casta and Renato Dulbecco, all of eighty-five, an eminent medical scientist who'd won the Nobel Prize for his research into cancer.

The morning after the show, Casta cooed that she was missing Dulbecco, who had slowdanced the voluptuous Corsican-born model on the final night of the festival to the strains of 'La Vie en Rose'.

His conveniently scientific reaction to his young admirer's crush? 'I would gladly clone her,' he said. No one took offence. Again, that's Italy! Any country that could put a pouting young model alongside an internationally acclaimed research scientist as co-hosts of a hugely watched television music program has got to have something going for it. With that sort of nutty bravery, if Italy has anything to say about anything — including politics and economics — we should probably listen. Tongue in or out of the cheek, it's ultimately to do with attitude, values, definitions, aspirations, expectations, what feels good, and what seems right — and it works, at least for Italians.

Life, Love and the Pursuit of Religious Paradox

'We love life,' Italians keep telling you, whenever and wherever you find them. North, South, well-off or struggling, practising Catholic, lapsed or never-have-been, they practically apologise when they say it. Maybe it's uttered as an explanation for a lot of individual foibles and national characteristics that they fear you may not approve. As an outsider, you could well surmise that Italians loving life essentially means having a focus, a focus on a handful of priorities that most of them share. Football, food and politics are their most recognisable priorities, the three things that above all else they appear to cherish, a word very close to love. Indeed, these three apparent fundamentals of a contented life give both Italians and their observers a focal point, a way of referring to them and distinguishing them.

By conspicuous contrast, most other national or ethnic groupings — our lot, Australians, being a near-perfect example — can thrash about either individually and collectively over an entire lifetime, without ever really discovering their priorities, passions and focal points. Some die never knowing what is important to them. In Australia's case, for instance, this ambivalence has probably unconsciously scuppered fundamental decisions on vital national matters such as becoming a Republic, something the Italians have done twice, just to make sure!

Running a poor fourth to the 'big three' of football, food and politics is religion. Nominally 98 per cent Catholic, Italy is a religious country — if by religious we mean there are lots of churches and plenty of people attending them. But if by religious we mean that Italians abide by the catechisms, creeds, commandments and teachings of the Catholic Church, then Italy is not religious. But then again, Catholicism is not that kind of religion. Like neo-Buddhists who cover their failure base by guaranteeing themselves reincarnation in another life, Catholics get their second chance via the confession booth.

As a family of non-Catholics lazing away the 1999 European summer on the Adriatic coast, we faced our own religio-ethical dilemma in Otranto, Italy's easternmost town close to the tip of the Puglian heel. With its ancient Greek and Byzantine origins, Otranto boasts a beautiful eleventh-century cathedral, packed with artistic treasures including a Baroque facade, a Renaissance portal, a Gothic rose-window and fabulous mosaics.

Not unlike their parents, Ned and Serge are not immediately or identifiably religious but, pleasingly, they are interested in what goes with other people's beliefs. In Otranto's cathedral, Serge asked if he could go into a confession cubicle to see what it was like inside. At the time, there was no priest present taking confession, so we hesitated. We considered the circumstances and decided not to allow him into the empty booth. Something told us that, to others at least, it might have been regarded as sacrilegious. He was a little disappointed about it, so we told him he could maybe do it another time. Were we right or wrong? Would it have been sacrilegious or a sin? If it would have been a sin, it was a forgivable one.

The Catholic arrangement is the perfect arrangement. Do wrong, be cleansed as often as you like or at least as often as God's agent, the priest, will put up with your nagging failures and misdemeanours from adultery to leaving the washing out in the rain. It's possibly the ultimate contrary Italian ritual.

Coming from a country like Australia where there are really very few rituals, it's difficult to fully appreciate, let alone explain, the dominance of ritual in a society that has got them, like Italy. The most absorbing aspect of Italian rituals is their pervasiveness.

Throughout the country, the same rituals — from the ridiculous to the regal, from the silly to the sacred — occur every day. They touch just about every Italian. From the obligatory *cappuccino* and *dolce* that start the Italian day to the irresistible *passeggiata* most of them take every evening, they are the ties that bind all Italians. There's the hideous ritual of the protracted Italian schoolday from eight in the morning until five in the evening (for older kids, sometimes six days a week); the folkloric ritual of *calcio* — playing it, watching it and following it; the ritual of religion, of the Church, Catholicism, prayer, the local father and confession; the ritual of the arts, every Italian's personal possession; and of music. There's the ritual of *pranzo* at home and the *siesta* that follows, and the ritual of the working day that goes so late as a result. Then there's the ritual of the woman, of *mamme* and *nonne* respected and loved and other women who are lusted after. There's the ritual of the summer suntan and the abbreviated bikini; indeed, the ritual of overt Italian sensuality, of style and dressing — or undressing — to please yourself as much as anyone else, of *bella figura*, of looking good. Then there's the ritual of appearing to be incredibly sexy but remaining unavailable, and the other ritual of older women at home and younger women at work, bookended by that hugely traditional set of rituals connected to the family, of eating together, of only drinking alcohol with food, of wine as food, of pasta itself, of talking about the next meal while you're having the present one, of oil as elixir, of taking a box of *dolce* to Mamma's every Sunday morning, of Mamma preparing food for the married 'boy' to take home with him, even though his wife, his *moglie*, is a great cook. There's the pleasantly unavoidable ritual of the same-things market in the village or town square and the people you bump into there every week; the ritual of the bar, of going to the same one and meeting friends who just happen to find themselves there too; the ritual of where the girls go while the guys are at the bar; the ritual of where women in general go, while the men are still around; the old-new ritual of meeting in the medieval *centro*, where shaved heads and motorbike leathers mix with corduroy, polo shirts and pressed jeans; the ritual of the wives who don't appear to cheat and the husbands who definitely do; the ritual of the teenagers who smoke; the ritual of old men who meet in the *piazza*, same place, same time, every day, and the women who never do; the ritual of the stuff-up, the hold-up and the tedium of the bureaucracy; the ritual of the inevitable Italian double-standard; the ritual of condemning the government whatever its political persuasion that day; the ritual of not believing in change but embracing it; the ritual of being honest but avoiding paying your taxes at all costs; the ritual of the Mafia; the ritual of not always winning but somehow never losing; the ritual of having only one kid but not believing in contraception; the ritual of loving your kids but treating them a bit like adorable toys; the ritual of the annual *vacanza* by the sea, the umbrella, the deck chairs and the aquarobics; the ritual of *Pasqua*, Easter, and *Natale*, Christmas; the ritual of Church versus State and of the individual versus the nation; the ritual of walking the dog *and* your ageing Papà; the ritual of two old men on a park bench in the morning sun chatting about football, food and politics; the ritual of hanging around but eventually going home. Then there's the ritual that probably overshadows all Italian rituals, the ritual of the *passeggiata*, the obligatory evening stroll down the *corso*, which one honest San Giovannese friend admitted made about as much sense as Olympic swimming — 'dive in, get to the other end, turn around and come back again!' And, of course, there's the ultimate ritual — of being proudly Italian, even without being entirely sure what being Italian means.

So What Does Italy Really Have to Teach the World?

The more you think about what makes Italy what it is, the more obvious it becomes that its very combination of frustration, passion and paradox, which so baffles and intrigues, also endears and enlightens. When it comes to comparing Italy and Italians, as a people, as a nation and as a society to the rest of the world, don't bother. *Contrast* them.

At once, Italy is old and new, modern and medieval. It is corporate Fiat, ruthless Olivetti, simple farmer and subsistence agriculture. It is Catholic and Communist, the Pope and Marx. It is Left, Right and Centre. It is both urban and rural, North and South, rich and poor, wealth and deprivation. It is religious and sacrilegious, devout and blasphemous, committed and casual, spiritual and secular, Church and State. It is corruption and righteousness. It is bureaucracy and enterprise. It is public and private. It is callous and profit-motivated, humanitarian and giving. It is superficially physical and deeply aesthetic. It is football heroes and derided politicians. It is crowded and poky, open and enervating. It is morally repressive and unexpectedly liberal. It is funny and sad. It is chauvinistic male and liberated female. It is Mamma and mammaries. It is fidelity and infidelity. It is Puccini and late-night porn. It is self-important and self-satisfied, egalitarian and generous. It is family tradition and New Age independence. It is individualism and collectivism. It is ego and community. It is clangorous and rowdy, peaceful and tranquil. It is political and apolitical, democratic and disorganised. It is youth and age, kids and *nonne*. It is *carabinieri* and Mafia. It is insular and parochial. It is free, unrestrained and worldly, localised and far-sighted. It is dogmatic and flexible. It is friendly and welcoming, distant and inward. It is narrowly Italian and strangely expansive, nationalistic and humanistic. It is stylish and dishevelled, artistic and tacky. It is conscious and unconscious, contrived and natural. It is Mediterranean and cosmopolitan, Western and something else, European and international. It is fine food and fast crap, great wines and cheap junk. It is the filigreed architectural beauty of the past and concrete suburban eyesores of the present. It is classic fountains and ringing piazzas, polluted rivers and piles of garbage. It is industrial ugliness and artistic genius. It is the efficiency and danger of the *autostrade* and the infuriating snarl of constricted cobblestoned lanes. It is Verdi, Vivaldi and very ordinary rock'n'roll. It is Pavarotti and Pino Daniele.

But unlike so many other nationalities, Italians don't thrust their Italianness on you. They believe that *being* Italian — or even *doing* Italian or *sharing* Italian — is sufficiently desirable to be willingly sought. But there are many things in Italy that are negative and less than desirable. It is endemically corrupt, legalised and bureaucratised to the point of stagnation and utter frustration. It is hidebound by religion and even history, bedevilled by a petty disregard for the law, by organised crime and the remnants of the Mafia, cramped by ethnic tradition, and hindered by split morality that borders on hypocrisy as well as by its plethora of questionable individual attitudes and habits.

Italians are also infuriatingly arrogant about their achievements and can be completely intolerant of others with differing priorities. They find it difficult to openly acknowledge to others that they may have gotten any aspect of life wrong, even though within themselves they know they have. Educationally, they are old-fashioned and near moribund.

Many of them, both men and women, have turned infidelity into a pre-requisite for a happy marriage. They are sometimes inherently racist, most times sexist, and, on occasion, unequal, unfree, riven by division, disunity and factionalism.

Democratically, of course, they are, to say the least, doubtful. The majority of what they call television is fatuous nonsense, albeit usually harmless fatuous nonsense. The explicitness of their late-night, free-to-air, un-X-rated girlie programs would be banned in most other countries, as would the ads displayed openly in the half a dozen or more lingerie retailers in every town or village in the land.

But for all its faults, divisions, paradoxes and contradictions, its shortcomings and its double-standards, Italy works — if 'working' means that most Italians are relatively contented within the bounds of their own definition. Old social problems appear manageable; emerging new ones are recognised for what they are. Suicides are rare. Mental illness is at 'normal' levels. Alcoholism is difficult to find. Drug addiction has yet to really make an impact. Divorce rates are lower than comparable averages. Immigration — both legal and otherwise — is, for the most part, tolerable and tolerated. Small business is still at the heart of the country's microeconomy. Bankruptcy is not common. Tax avoidance is a national sport, but the mixed Italian economy continues to grow. Like everywhere else in the modern world, joblessness is a constant worry, more so in the neglected South, but even this is changing, slowly and in line with political interests. Crime rates are not high. Even the influence of the Mafia appears to be subsiding. Meanwhile, as one of the world's most desirable destinations, tourism continues to boom. Internationally and diplomatically, Italy's carefully cultivated image of co-operative independence is something to be envied. Political extremism and acts of terrorism still surface, but are largely controllable.

You could make the point that all is definitely not well in the Second Republic of Italy, but I'm sure most fair-minded citizens from other parts of the world would prefer to deal with Italy's defects rather than grapple with the ones they find in their own countries.

So how come Italy seems to survive, even thrive on its defects, almost in spite of itself? Why do Italians find it so easy to live with the country's infinite frustrations? Why does Italy prosper despite its questionable work ethic? Why is Italy able to conduct itself as an integral part of the wider global community despite its insularity and irritating self-importance? These questions I cannot answer. There is, however, an 'Italian way'. The Italians themselves call it *all'italiana*. However I or they explain it, this celebrated 'Italian way' of going about things as individuals and as a country is both infuriatingly wrong and surprisingly right. 'Football, food and politics ... all the rest is mere detail!' Disagree if you like, but no Italian I've met has.

Winter in Campiglia

In early January 2000, courtesy of particularly generous friends, I lucked onto Campiglia Marittima, an enchanting hill town on the Etruscan coast, as a suitably tranquil place to finish off this book. Remote in its own way but not all that far from Pisa and its lucratively leaning tower, one of Campiglia's most enticing attributes was that I'd never heard of it. At least not until our new mates Aldo and Ann, an Italo-Australian couple from Strada-in-Chianti, suggested I borrow their cosy holiday apartment on the postage-stamp-sized Piazza Mazanni in its medieval *centro storico*.

As hill towns go, Campiglia Marittima is about as exquisitely Italian as they get. Restfully overlooking the sea on a ridge back from the nearby coast, it's quaint but not twee, carefully restored but neither modified nor unnecessarily modernised. Its narrow lanes were never made for vehicles but somehow the locals still manage to get them in and out of the most impossibly confined spaces. The piazzas are small but lively; its stone and brick buildings all the same but unique in their own way; the people, in winter at least, mainly Italians who don't seem to do a lot other than live there. If it were a hundred kilometres away to the east nearer to Florence or in the sought-after Chianti Hills, not only would its real estate be astronomically expensive, Campiglia Marittima would be overrun by foreigners carrying thick chequebooks.

On a clear day — as the Campiglia locals will always tell you — from the wall that semi-circles the town on its downward side you can make out the islands of the Tuscan archipelago. But on the day I peered out from my window to the coast beyond, everything had that hazy Italian winter look, from Campiglia's hill-top vantage point down the wooded slopes, through cherished private vineyards and the patchwork olive groves with their rumbling tractor-trailers and chit-chatting farm workers, over the next hill with its *chiesa*, past the next knoll with its converted *palazzo*, the extensively farmed plains, the inevitable urban ugliness of San Vincenzo's powerhouses and factories and eventually to the misty sheen of the Tuscan Gulf with its islands silhouetted in the afternoon sun. An armada of moored freighters was only just discernible. There's a lot of Italy in one panoramic 270 degree sweep. Indeed, there's a lot of Italy in Campiglia Marittima without even taking in its spectacular views to the north, south and east.

Ann assured me it would be good fun to take a stroll around the village. She was right. Mornings and afternoons, I exercised my cramped legs and word-cluttered brain in and around its bewildering maze of concentric semi-circles, unusual even for centuries-old Italian hill towns. Most of them are cobbled or paved and so poky they've been closed to traffic. Only those three-wheeled api mini-trucks can negotiate their steepness and barely head-high arches. Sounds as well as sights make places like Campiglia Marittima so serene — a gentle breeze through the pines, the low murmur of conversations from behind stone walls.

Campiglia was not only fun and fascinating, it was also a sign of changing Italian times. Of late, many of its old houses have been purchased by Swiss, French, and what the locals call 'Florentine foreigners', Italians from that 'elsewhere Italy'. Luckily, they weren't around in the chilly winter months while I was there. They're definitely fairweather-only Campigliese.

That winter, it felt like I was the only stranger in town, and I think I was. At least that's the way the locals treated me when I went to the bar, the *macelleria*, the *giornalaio* and the *alimentari* — friendly enough but curious. It wasn't so much a case of 'What's he doing here?', rather 'I wonder what he's doing here?'. But a couple of morning *macchiati*, some shopping and an evening watching Fiorentina versus AC Milan on TV in the Bar Bacco and their early caution gave way to tacit acceptance — 'Oh, that guy — an Australian, somebody said — he's still around.' Acceptance, by the way, is possibly a trifle presumptuous. Friendly acknowledgment is closer to the mark.

Campiglia goes back a long way, which is a non-historian's trite way of saying over a thousand years. It's steeped in history, yet in this out-of-the-way Tuscan hill town, the new and the old seem to co-exist, to live together easily. For instance, Campiglia has the Rocca di San Silvestro, the ruins of an abandoned twelfth-century mining village. After all of eight hundred years it still dominates the town from above the Valle dei Manienti. But just below, near the main piazza, there's a pinball parlour. It also has a majestic bell tower that woke me every morning at six; car radios blaring Italian pop music by the likes of Jovanotti and Ligabue kept me awake every night until close to midnight. The ends of the Italian time tunnel are never very far apart, despite the centuries and eras between them. You can't help thinking that because they live physically side-by-side with the past, Italians appear to be more confident with the present and less nervous or intimidated by their uncertain future. Susan Cahill put it marvellously in *Desiring Italy* when she said that 'Italians have the courage of their contradictions'.

A few unforeseen personal-cum-professional hiccups back home in Australia meant that my first writing week in Campiglia was, to say the least, mixed. Away from my loved ones, there were times when I felt a bit outside myself. Uncharacteristically, for a short while I was incapable of either influencing or correcting nasty elements plaguing our family existence, mine in particular.

The details are irrelevant, but there were moments when I was almost glad to be alone and unable to throw my weight around in the direction of distant adversaries, to be at a distance from the sources of our distress. On the other hand, there were moments when I craved compatibility and closeness. I was being called upon to handle extremes of emotion. I was sad yet happy, angry yet understanding, depressed yet divorced.

Looking out of my apartment window over a terracotta jigsaw of red-, orange-, yellow- and ochre-tiled rooftops, straight, curved, on assorted levels and planes, all over the shop but with a sort of bizarre symmetry, a magical mess of intentional and unintentional Italian beauty, I longed for Kirsty to be able to capture on film what I was seeing with my own eyes, and to have my family with me. I might have actually copped a dose of the 'yins and yangs' myself. Maybe I had become temporarily Italian? But then again, I didn't have 'the courage of my contradictions'. Unlike the vast majority of Italians, the rest of us seem hellbent on straightening out our contradictions, rather than learning to live with them. Our chances of enjoying them, benefiting from them, are close to minimal. Perhaps you have to be born contradictory like the Italians.

I don't know whether I will ever go back to Campiglia. But if I don't, I've taken a lot from it, including memories of both desperation and elation. I experienced a personal kind of 'Third Way' in Campiglia — not happiness, not sadness, but something curiously in between.

The New Economy and Italy

As I looked around at the world from Italy, Communism and the Left were, by all accounts, defunct. In the so-called 'New World Order', ideological differences were supposed to be no longer here nor there. Some in fact argued that they were already obsolete, that ideology itself was no more — 'the end of history' and all that rubbish.

The market and its mates, so we were all being told ad nauseam, would rule unchallenged and indefinitely. Democracy was a given, eagerly sought by all. Governments would continue to shrink. Globalisation was inevitable and unavoidable. Deregulation and privatisation were buzzwords, economic rationalism and marketism widely accepted as the only ways to go. The Internet was both the answer to all our prayers and the one and only truly democratic vehicle. Private dot coms would succeed where public institutions had failed.

The new economy had taken precedence over politics itself. Free trade would get nothing but freer. The old tried and failed 'trickle-down' effect would become a veritable torrent in its new global guise. Everyone, everywhere, we were assured, would benefit. Bill Gates was the icon of the times, the Internet touted as the cure for everything from the common cold to cancer, from poverty to pornography. The click of a mouse would see billions of dollars per second hurtling meteor-like through the global money market. The world and the human race would instantly be rid of its social ills. Life — without government interference and ideological debate — was, thanks to cybertechnology and globalisation, finally going to be perfectible. For the want of a more derogatory verbal blast, hogwash and humbug! The events of 1999 and 2000 proved just how harebrained the new certitudes of the techno-global Right were, pretty much like all the old ones propounded by dogmatic Left before them.

What has all this got to do with Italy, Italian politics and the so-called 'Italian way'? The answer is really a question, or a series of interrelated questions. Have you ever wondered why Italy is one of the most visited countries on Earth? It can't be just the food and the football, as marvellous as they might be. Maybe the Italians' approach to life and politics — as distinct from their actual execution of it — has something to do with it, albeit subliminally. A scoreable goal, a cookable meal and winnable politics as a formula for a whole lot more? This is how Italian journalist Beppi Severgnini put what he regards as *the* single greatest principle regulating Italian public life: 'If you see a hurdle, walk around it. Trying to jump is too tiring!'

What else is there to be said?

The Third Way — Ideology or Lifestyle?

There are people out there who will tell you that the Third Way phenomenon is not really a political thing, that it's more about lifestyle. This is somehow offered as a criticism, as though seeking 'lifestyle' is an undesirable political activity.

But these critics are missing a terrifyingly basic point. What the hell is politics about if it's not ultimately about lifestyle? Ditto economics and sociology. In themselves, for their own sakes, these unstoppable human pursuits make absolutely no sense. Sense only comes when politics and economics convert into lifestyle, into what we laughingly used to call 'society', what we actually do with ourselves on a daily basis, what we are able to make of our lives, individually and collectively. Aren't lifestyle and politics one and the same? If they're not, they bloody well should be! When Third Wayers question what we get out of the Left or the Right, they are really questioning their capacity to deliver 'lifestyle' — for the few or the many. Look at the Italians. Does anyone dispute that they have one of the most enviable lifestyles in the world? And even though they've turned compromise into a political art form, is not the Italian economy consistently one the world's strongest?

Città Slow — Progressive Regression

We didn't have to look very far from our temporary Tuscan home of San Giovanni Valdarno to find a quintessentially Italian version of what a fresh start to the twenty-first century might look like.

In October 1999, thirty-six towns and cities spread throughout the length and breadth of Italy declared they were so fed up with the pace of modern life that they'd joined forces 'in a drive to make it slower'. So much for those who believe progress must mean faster and that slower must mean slacker! Progressive regression is one way you could describe what they were getting at; they dubbed it Città Slow, or Slow Cities, an offshoot of the well-established Slow Food.

Unapologetic and uncomplicated, the aim of Slow Cities is to preserve the traditional Italian way of life, so distinct and deeply rooted in regions like Tuscany, Umbria, Abruzzo, the Amalfi Coast and others. The founding Città Slow members included wonderful hill towns such as Urbino, Todi, Orvieto and Asti, and incomparably beautiful but still largely unspoiled coastal villages like Positano, on the Amalfi Coast south of Naples. The movement is led by Paolo Saturnini, the mayor of the classically Tuscan *paese* of Greve-in-Chianti, only about thirty kilometres through the Chianti Hills from San Giovanni Valdarno. The good burghers of Città Slow say they are determined to 'set an example to others enslaved by unbridled modernism'.

So what exactly have these unanimously proud Italian towns decided to do? How do they intend taking on the might of globalisation, so-called 'progress'? Well, for something that is in itself so political, even philosophical, the Città Slow modus operandi is immensely practical. Take, for example, that great contemporary bugbear, traffic. The Città Slow plan is to completely rid *centri storichi* of all vehicles. Residents and tourists are encouraged to rent and ride bicycles, and fleets of quiet, non-polluting electrically powered buses will be introduced where they don't already exist. Gone are television antennae and all other aerials on roofs, replaced by underground cables. Buildings regarded as 'ugly modern architecture' are bulldozed to the ground.

Under the plan to move backwards to go forwards, town residents are urged to grow sweet-smelling plants. Well-laid council schemes are in place to preserve and promote local craft and artisans' shops, rapidly disappearing sights in contemporary Italy. Città Slow restaurants offer only the freshest local produce and specialities. Not unsurprisingly in the current climate, local production of genetically modified food is banned.

It would be simplistic, in fact it would be missing the point completely, to write off Città Slow as a pack of neo-Luddites. Paolo Saturnini told London's *Daily Telegraph*: 'In the world in which we live, we leave ever less time for reflection, free time, the pleasures of life — last but not least among them, that of food. Towns are becoming more besieged by cars, noise and air pollution. More and more they are coming to resemble one another. McDonald's and the same franchise outlets for pullovers, jeans, shoes, telephones and even bread are taking over everywhere.'

For so long Italy was a nation of thousands of towns 'with their own mark, identity, culture and traditions', but today, great chunks of what had been a visually and culturally distinctive land have 'come to resemble Las Vegas'. But the prognosis is not all gloomy. Other parts of Italy have fortunately been spared and Città Slow wants to keep it that way. Heretics of the modern world they might be, but as far as they see it, preservation and progress are not mutually exclusive.

What Città Slow are advocating, indeed what Italy has demonstrated with varying degrees of success for thousands of years, is that the way to go forward is to consciously embrace the past, the present and the future, to mix the global and the local and, as the good mayor himself put it, to move towards 'a marriage of tradition and the very best of technological innovation'. 'Same dough, different loaf,' as my very wise old Italian friend put it. An Italian recipe for the Third Way? As I've been harping on throughout this book, the Italians have always got a lot more than just their football and their food right ...

As Matt Frei writes in *Italy: The Unfinished Revolution*, his attempt to explain the Italian unexplainable, Italian society is nowhere near as chaotic and haphazard as it might appear: 'Take the enjoyable and deceptively simple act of drinking a cappuccino. This ritual is a minefield of regulations — rule number one, never have a cappuccino after eleven in the morning; rule number two, never order a cappuccino after lunch or dinner; rule number three, never have your cappuccino sitting down!'

Any nation that has thought that long and hard about when and how to drink coffee should be listened to! Have you ever drunk better coffee than Italian coffee? Unlikely. So if the Italians say there's a Third Way out there to make the politically unworkable work, who are we to argue?

Ossimoro

It was an unseasonably mild evening. We were in Aldo's Preludio bar, our favourite San Giovannese watering-hole, mainly because it's right in the thick of things on the Piazza Masaccio. There we were sipping *prosecco* — a cheeky little sparkling Italian *vino bianco* that we'd taken quite a fancy to, sweeter than real champagne, but thankfully a hell of a lot drier than the dreaded spumante, not Italy's finest gift to the world's wine lovers — and talking with Lucio Cavicchioli, an observant English-speaking local friend who'd lived and worked in the Italian Embassy in Canberra and married Marissa, an Italo-Australian. At one point I asked arguably the most stupid question I've ever asked, either professionally or off-duty.

'Lucio,' I said, 'what is it about Italians?'

As so many Italians can and do when you're looking for a simple answer to a complex question, Lucio had a word for it: 'We have a *parola* — *ossimoro*. *Ossimoro* means sort of opposites, contradiction — like *amore* and *odio*, love and hate.'

'You know,' I found myself musing into my *bicchiere di prosecco*, 'it sounds to me like this word of yours, *ossimoro* — if you'll pardon my pronunciation — is pretty close to a working definition of this entire country and its bloody people. You've worked out how to live with opposites. Contradictions don't faze you. To use your love-hate example, it doesn't seem to bother you in the slightest that you all love this country yet every single one of you rubbishes it, perpetually, to the point of near-hatred. That's actually life to you lot, not contradiction. That's the paradox. That's why you also have such an amazing capacity for compromise — bloody *ossimoro*! Thanks, Lucio. Your buy.'

Back at our apartment by the sluggish Arno, I dived for the dictionary and the hit the thesaurus key on the lap-top at the same time. The English word I was after was 'oxymoron', one of those eccentric isolated remnants of learning that stay with you, curious recollections from high-school English classes.

If the Italians are to be believed, if their instinctive 'Italian Way' does have applications elsewhere, then the true definition of *ossimoro* — the conjunction of contradiction — will have to be accepted as the template for making all things political, economic and social workable, even enjoyable. If perfection in politics is unattainable — and it would be bloody boring if it was — improving on its imperfections has to be the next best thing. Why waste precious time in the dull pursuit of one defective ideology after another from the Left or the Right, when the pursuit of an amalgam of the two might produce the goods?

Back in 1960, when Anita Ekberg, in Federico Fellini's *La Dolce Vita*, frolicked wet and low-cut in Rome's Trevi Fountain, she seemed to capture the essence, the attitude, the spirit of the Italian people. Italians did indeed enjoy *la dolce vita*, 'the sweet life'. Today, however, it could be argued that *La Dolce Vita* has given way to *La Terza Via*. Feel absolutely free, as many of you will, to disagree. That's the idea, the purpose of the exercise — to provoke a convivial yelling match in a local bar over a *birra*, *vino*, *grappa* or *caffè*. If you can drag the conversation away from football, food and politics, then the bar you are in is most assuredly not Italian.

Acknowledgments

The author's fifteen months of almost religious reading of the *International Herald Tribune* and its daily lift-out, *Italy Daily*, provided not only ideas and story lines, but heaps of back-up information, even confirmation of his own theories and prejudices. This being the case, it would be hugely remiss of me not to acknowledge the many *IHT* and *ID* writers and contributors who prodded my 'Italophilic' mental meandering. Thanks, in particular, to the *IHT*'s Milan-based Managing Editor, Gabriel Kahn, for his personal OK to 'lift' the bits we have. As promised, a copy of *The World from Italy: Football, Food and Politics* is in the mail!

IHT and *ID* source writers and contributors: Stefano Salimbeni, Christopher Emsden, John Vinocur, Rob Hughes (*London Times*), David Nyham (*Boston Globe*), Laura Collura, Giorgio Tosatti (*Corriere della Sera*), Nicholas Rigillo, Kathryn Hone, Ann Swardson (*Washington Post*), Paul Auster (*Corriere della Sera/The New York Times*), Alfredo Pieroni (*Corriere della Sera*), Steve Pagani (*Reuters*), Donata Righetti (*Corriere della Sera*), Beppi Severgnini and

Indro Montanelli. Thanks also to Martin Kettle and Larry Elliott from *The Guardian* and Thomas Friedman from *The New York Times*.

Mille grazie to all our much-missed friends in San Giovanni Valdarno and elsewhere in Italy who prompted the daily thoughts and reactions that eventually found their way into these pages — Maddelana, Ann and Aldo, Beppi and Zita, Rossella, Alessio and Giulia, Simona and Samuele, Peter, everyone at *Il Sillabo* Language School (especially Anna Paula, Erica and Caterina), Stefano and Anna Maria at our pined-for *Locanda Cuccuini*, Cirro and Diana, Lisa and Paulo, Lucio and Marissa, Lorella and Damiano, Valleverde's Daniella and Fiorella, Ned's *allenatore* Pietro, Marco, Anna Maria and Fillipo, Barbara, David, Mattia, Romano and Anna, *il giornalaio* Pietro, Bette Ann Bierwirth, Marchese Piero di Antinori, Diana and Sergio, Silvano and Jean at Villa Massa, Aldo and the girls at *Preludio*, Massimo and the girls from the *focaceria Pane e Dintorni*, Isabella, Marcello, Francesco and Amelia, Graziano and Antonella, Keith and Helen, Lucia and Pippo, Catherine and Adriano on the outskirts of Roma, Gori's Gastronomia, the Gelateria L'Oasis in Montevarchi, the welcoming families and officials at the AC San Giovannese, Italo-Irish journo mate, Sean Salsarola — and the plethora of other generous and fascinating *Italiani* who made our dream come true, even those nightmarish bits about which other people write very different kinds of books.

ACKNOWLEDGMENTS

Ta to Rory Steele, Australian Ambassador to Italy; the Italian Ambassador to Australia, His Excellency Ambassador Giovanni Castellanata, and Chris Butler, 'Australian Ambassador to Montegonzi AR'; Janie Lalor; Rob Hill-Smith; Meryl and Andrea at Co.As.It; the teaching staff and parents, especially class 'carer' Laura at Serge's *Scuola Elementare Giorgio La Pira* and Manzo, Edi, Sergio, Sandra and the Signora President at Ned's *Scuola Media Marconi*; Roberto from the SGV Pro Loco; Piero from the *comune di SGV*; Mauro from the *Polizia Municipale*; fellow temporary Italian, Professor Wojciech Sadurski and his family; Don Di Fabrizio and his Abruzzese rellies for our summer vacation; Fritz, Costanza and their boys for the time in both Puglia and East Jerusalem; and Sig. G. Luck, formerly of Paciano, Umbria, for his exceptional nit-picking.

And, of course, it would be remiss of me not to thank my editor at HarperCollins, Jesse Fink. A fellow soccer nut, it was Jesse's bloody idea that yours truly should even think about a book in between football matches and pretending we were Italian. The end result has gone a little further than *calcio* — and he doesn't seem to mind. Journalists get pretty toey about other people fiddling about with their purple and even their not-so-purple prose, but you 'fiddled well', Jess!

Kirsty's and my appreciation to Jill Hickson for her early encouragement, and of course to Fiona Inglis from Curtis Brown for her 'literary handholding' — and what a relief that you had the original floppy from San Giovanni Valdarno in your top drawer!

And how could the boys keep up their *lingua italiana* without our town's resident *napoletana*, Beatrice, and Peter?

Thanks must also go to *tutti tifosi* in the *Curva Marioni* and *Curva Fiesole* — particularly Pierluigi and Riccardo; the helpful folk at FILA in Italy and Australia; the heart-stopping Gabriel Batistuta, Rui Costa, Francesco Toldo, Paul Okon, of course, and the other *calciatori* at AC Fiorentina — *Forza Viola!*; our good mate, Craig Johnston, for introducing us to Fiorentina and *l'ultima tifosa* Franca Smarelli.

Lateral gratitude also to Pino Daniele, Nek, Jovanotti, Giorgia, Ligabue, Adriano Celentano and Andrea Bocelli who made us feel 'musically Italian'; model and actor Megan Gale for giving us the opportunity to tell everyone that the 'perfect Italian woman' was actually Australian.

Acknowledgment 'gongs' too for every Italian chef and cook who delighted us; every Italian wine-maker who seduced us; every Italian caffè bar owner who stimulated us and every Italian politician who intrigued us.

Source Reading

So many thoughtful books have been written about the Italian 'thing', that the author feels in quite awesome company. What follows are those that I either read or at least scanned in the name of brain-picking. Where I have borrowed from any of their material — deliberately or subconsciously, via quotes or indirectly — the journalist in me has attributed same.

Jack Altman, *Discover Italy*, Berlitz Travel Guides

Luigi Barzini, *The Italians*, Atheneum, UK, 1996

Susan Cahill, *Desiring Italy*, Ballantine Books, New York, 1997

David Dale, *The 100 Things Everyone Needs to Know About Italy*, Pan MacMillan, Sydney, 1998

Matt Frei, *Italy: The Unfinished Revolution*, Mandarin Paperbacks, London, 1997

Thomas Friedman, *The Lexus and the Olive Tree*, HarperCollins, London, 2000

Anthony Giddens, *The Third Way*, Polity Press, Cambridge, UK, 1999

Valentina Harris, *Risotto! Risotto!*, Cassell Academic, 1999

John Haycraft, *Italian Labyrinth*, Penguin Books, Middlesex, 1985

Paul Hofmann, *That Fine Italian Hand*, Henry Holt, New York, 1990

Italy, Lonely Planet, Melbourne, 1996

Hans-Peter Martin, *The Global Trap*, Pluto Press, Australia, 1997

Jan Morris, *The World of Venice*, Faber & Faber, London, 1983

Roberto Nobbio, *Left and Right*, Polity Press, Cambridge, UK, 1996

P. J. O'Rourke, *Eat the Rich*, Atlantic Monthly Press, New York, 1998

Tim Parks, *An Italian Education*, Avon Books, UK, 1996

Tim Parks, *Italian Neighbours*, Fawcett Books, UK, 1993

Carlo Petrini, *The Slow Food Movement Manifesto*, Rome

Fred Plotkin, *Italy for the Gourmet Traveller*, Kyle Cathie, London, 1996

Alice Leccese Powers, *Italy in Mind*, Vintage Books, New York, 1997

Charles Richards, *The New Italians*, Penguin, Middlesex, 1995